Quotati

Vietnam: 19

"Some of the things which I shall say will repeat what has been said before, but memories here and abroad seem to be sometimes short."

Dean Rusk
Secretary of State
Washington, D.C.
February 25, 1965

"For most Americans this is an easy war. Men fight and men suffer and men die, as they always do in war. But the lives of most of us in this room and those listening to me this morning are untroubled. Prosperity rises, abundance increases, the nation flourishes."

Lyndon B. Johnson
President of the United States
Washington, D.C.
May 13, 1965

1283

Quotations

VIETNAM:

1945-1970

Compiled by William G. Effros

RANDOM HOUSE New York

Contents

	EDITOR'S NOTE	1
1	WHAT'S GOING ON THERE?	3
2	HOW DID WE GET INTO IT?	13
3	WHY ARE WE THERE?	30
	General	30
	The Domino Theory	46
	SEATO	53
	Aggression from the North	57
4	WHO'S WINNING?	62
	1950 to the Geneva Agreements	62
	The Geneva Agreements to Tet 1968	72
	After Tet 1968	92
5	THE TONKIN INCIDENT	98
6	THE TONKIN RESOLUTION	102
7	BOMBING	107
8	"WE SEEK NO WIDER WAR"	117

9 WHEN WILL THEY ATTACK
   AGAIN?   124

10 THE GENEVA AGREEMENTS   128

11 ''THE LEGAL GOVERNMENT
    OF VIETNAM''   134

12 HO CHI MINH   146

13 ''AMERICA'S FINEST
    HOUR''   149

14 PLANS TO END THE WAR   158
    Negotiations   158
    Vietnamization   169
    Withdrawal   191
    Military Solutions   202
    *"The Exact Plan Must Be Kept
    Secret for Now"*   218

15 THE SILENT MAJORITY   221

16 LAOS   227

17 CAMBODIA   236

    INDEX   245

Editor's Note

The quotes selected for this book represent samples of all published viewpoints on the Vietnam conflict. Quotes are in context and reflect the views of the speaker at the time he made the statement.

W.G.E.

What's Going On There?

"There are some parts of the world where people are not allowed to hear the truth because the governments are afraid to let the people know the facts."

Philip C. Jessup
United States Ambassador to Indochina
August 13, 1950

"The time has come for the American people to be told the blunt truth about Indochina."

John F. Kennedy
Senator from Massachusetts
Washington, D.C.
April 6, 1954

"What is American policy on Indochina?"

"All of us have listened to the dismal series of reversals and confusions and alarms and excursions which have emerged from Washington over the past few weeks."

Lyndon B. Johnson
Senate Minority Leader
Washington, D.C.
May 6, 1954

"We will insist upon clear explanations of the policies in which we are asked to cooperate. We will insist that we and the American people be treated as adults—that we have the facts without sugar coating . . ."

Lyndon B. Johnson
Senate Minority Leader
May 17, 1954

"The United States is now involved in an undeclared war in South Vietnam. This is well known to the Russians, the Chinese Communists, and everybody else concerned except the American people."

James Reston
New York Times
Washington, D.C.
February 13, 1962

"The people should not have to wait until American casualty lists are posted before being informed about the real nature of the nation's commitment to South Vietnam. We would ask President Kennedy to drop the pretense that the United States is merely acting as military advisor to South Vietnam."

Battle Line
Publication of the Republican National Committee
Washington, D.C.
February 13, 1962

"Your approach to the questions of the press should emphasize the positive aspects of your activities and avoid gratuitous criticism . . .

"As songwriter Johnny Mercer put it, you've got to accentuate the positive and eliminate the negative."

U.S. Army briefing given to all servicemen going to
South Vietnam
Prepared by United States Continental Command
Fort Monroe, Virginia

"In recent weeks the American public has been surprised by developments in Vietnam—developments which have been many months in the making but which the American people are just now discovering.

"The restrictive United States press policy in Vietnam . . . unquestionably contributed to the lack of information about conditions in Vietnam which created an international crisis.

"Instead of hiding the facts from the American public, the State Department should have done everything possible to expose the true situation to full view."

John E. Moss
Chairman of the House Government Information
    Subcommittee
Washington, D.C.
September 30, 1963

"I think the American public has been given a very full picture of what's going on both by the government and by the press."

George W. Ball
Under Secretary of State
Voice of America radio broadcast
May 16, 1964

"Editors of this country do object to the contradictions, the double talk and half truths that the press is getting both in Washington and Saigon.

"In an undeclared war, the United States press in Vietnam faces stronger restrictions than it ever has in wartime.

"The people of the United States deserve to be well informed in this crisis no matter how negative the news might be.

"We fear it is not getting the full story nor the true story at this time."

George Beebe
President of the Associated Press Managing Editors
    Association
Miami, Florida
April 20, 1965

" 'I [said Arthur Sylvester, Assistant Secretary of Defense for Public Affairs] can't understand how you fellows can write what you do while American boys are dying out here.'

"Then he went on to the effect that American correspondents had a patriotic duty to disseminate only information that made the United States look good.

"A network television correspondent said, 'Surely, Arthur, you don't expect the American press to be handmaidens of government.'

" 'That's exactly what I expect,' came the reply.

"An agency man raised the problem that had preoccupied Ambassador Taylor and Barry Zorthian—about the credibility of American officials. Responded the Assistant Secretary of Defense for Public Affairs:

" 'Look, if you think any American official is going to tell you the truth, then you're stupid. Did you hear that?—Stupid.' "

Morely Safer
Dateline 1966
Publication of the Overseas Press Club of America
Conversation took place in Saigon, July 17, 1965

"The fault lies in great part with an administration that fails to inform the people fully and frankly about the objectives and progress of the war."

Melvin R. Laird
House Minority Leader
Washington, D.C.
April 30, 1966

"I just had the greatest brainwashing that anyone can get when you go over to Vietnam, not only by the generals, but also by the diplomatic corps over there, and they do a very thorough job."

George Romney
Governor of Michigan
Detroit, Michigan
September 4, 1967

"He was a farm boy who had worked in the fields, and his family just didn't believe sunstroke killed him.

"I checked into it, and the Pentagon reported his face and body were reddened by the sun while he waited three hours to be evacuated by helicopter from combat.

"Finally they acknowledged he was waiting to be evacuated because he had three bullet holes in him. And they call that an incidental death! Well, they changed it.

"The number of combat killed and wounded have become so great—only the world wars were more deadly in recent history—they are trying to hide it . . . a clumsy effort to deceive the public about casualities in this most unpopular and undeclared war."

Stephen M. Young
Senator from Ohio
Washington, D.C.
April 29, 1969

"I believe that one of the reasons for the deep
division about Vietnam is that many Americans
have lost confidence in what the government has
told them about our policy. The American people
cannot and should not be asked to support a
policy which involves the overriding issues of war
and peace unless they know the truth about that
policy."

  Richard M. Nixon
  President of the United States
  Washington, D.C.
  November 3, 1969

"I believe that the nation is being misled over the
issues at stake in Vietnam as it was in 1966 and
1967."

  Eugene J. McCarthy
  Senator from Minnesota
  Washington, D.C.
  February 19, 1970

How Did We Get Into It?

"There have been no requests, suggestions, nor plans for sending American military units to Indo-China."

Major General Graves B. Erskine
Commander, First U.S. Marine Division
Ranking Defense Department representative with the
United States mission studying problems of military
aid to the French Union States of Indochina
July 20, 1950

"I would never send troops there."

Dwight D. Eisenhower
General, United States Army
New York City
June 8, 1952

"The United States has military missions in Indo-China."

Dwight D. Eisenhower
President of the United States
Washington, D.C.
February 3, 1954

"I can give categorical assurances that there is no intention of sending those two divisions or any other to Indo-China.

"[The dispatch of two hundred Air Force technicians] in no way indicates a desire or intent to send any ground forces to that part of the world."

William F. Knowland
Senate Majority Leader
Washington, D.C.
February 8, 1954

"I can conceive of no greater tragedy than for the United States to become involved in an all-out war in Indo-China."

Dwight D. Eisenhower
President of the United States
Washington, D.C.
February 10, 1954

"I renew my protest. I renew my request that our Air Force mechanics be withdrawn from Indo-China. For the good they do, the risk is too great . . . We are taking steps that lead our men directly into combat . . . soon we may have to fight or run."

John C. Stennis
Member of the Senate Armed Services Committee
Washington, D.C.
March 9, 1954

"There is going to be no involvement of America in war unless it is a result of the Constitutional process that is placed upon Congress to declare it. Now let us have that clear."

Dwight D. Eisenhower
President of the United States
Washington, D.C.
March 10, 1954

"The United States is carrying 78 percent of the cost of the Indo-Chinese war."

Christian Pineau
Deputy in the French National Assembly
Paris, France
March 16, 1954

"It is hoped that the United States will not have to send troops there, but if this government cannot avoid it, the administration must face up to the situation and dispatch forces."

Richard M. Nixon
Vice-President of the United States
Washington, D.C.
April 16, 1954

"It is my belief that prior to commitment of any armed forces—land, sea or air—the President would and should come to Congress and lay the facts before it with his recommendations."

William F. Knowland
Senate Majority Leader
Washington, D.C.
April 17, 1954

"We must not permit a single American to be drafted and sent to fight in the jungles of Indo-China."

William E. Jenner
Senator from Indiana
Washington, D.C.
April 20, 1954

"We have intervened in that war. They might just as well say we are in the war now."

Usher L. Burdick
Representative from North Dakota
Washington, D.C.
April 21, 1954

"We would not get into a war except through Constitutional process, which, of course, involves the declaration of war by Congress."

Dwight D. Eisenhower
President of the United States
Washington, D.C.
April 29, 1954

"Only Congress can declare war."

John Foster Dulles
Secretary of State
Washington, D.C.
May 7, 1954

"Using United States ground forces in the Indo-China jungle would be like trying to cover an elephant with a handkerchief—you just can't do it."

William F. Knowland
Senate Majority Leader
Washington, D.C.
May 16, 1954

"The Vietnamese have ample manpower and even today outnumber the enemy by 100,000, with superior firepower at least in a ratio of two to one and probably more.

"We are ready to assist them in training an adequate national army for the security of their homeland . . .

"[The war can be won] without bringing in one single American soldier to fight."

General John W. O'Daniel
Head of the United States Military Mission
Saigon, South Vietnam
July 7, 1954

"We have exactly 342 men, the number allowed by the Geneva Armistice Conference. It would be a breeze if we had more."

General Samuel T. Williams
Head of the United States Advisory Group
Saigon, South Vietnam
June 12, 1957

"I don't agree at all with any partisan or other criticism of the United States build-up in Vietnam. My only question is whether it may be too little and too late. It is essential that the United States commit all the resources of which it is capable to avoid a Communist take-over in South Vietnam and the rest of Southeast Asia.

"I support President Kennedy to the hilt and I only hope he will step up the build-up and under no circumstances curtail it because of possible criticism."

Richard M. Nixon
Former Vice-President of the United States
Sacramento, California
February 15, 1962

"I would go to Congress before committing combat troops."

John F. Kennedy
President of the United States
Washington, D.C.
March 14, 1962

"The death of three American flyers and the injury of another this week revealed to the American people what the Communists have known for a long time—that United States Air Force planes, manned by United States pilots, as well as many Army light planes and helicopters have been engaged in active combat against the Vietminh guerrillas."

Editorial
New York Times
October 17, 1962

"I do not believe under certain circumstance a greater job could be done, to use your words, 'in Vietnam' with the introduction of U.S. combat forces. I say that because this is a war against realists. It is a war which depends for success upon support from local people primarily.

"So I really personally believe the introduction of U.S. ground troops in South Vietnam today would hinder rather than help the campaign against the insurgency."

Robert S. McNamara
Secretary of Defense
Washington, D.C.
February 17, 1964

"I would oppose the use of United States troops as the direct means of supressing the guerrillas in South Vietnam."

General Maxwell D. Taylor
Chairman, Joint Chiefs of Staff
Washington, D.C.
February 17, 1964

"I don't know what the U.S. is doing. They tell you people we're just in a training situation and they try to run us as a training base. But we're at war, we are doing the flying and fighting. We are losing. Morale is very bad . . .

"I'll bet you that anyone you talk to does not know that American pilots fight this war . . . The Vietnamese 'students' we have on board are airmen basics [recruits] . . . the only reason they are on board is in case we crash there is one American 'advisor' and one Vietnamese 'student' . . . they are sacrificial lambs . . . and they are a menace to have on board."

Letter from Air Force Captain Edwin G. Shank, Jr.
Dated January 20, 1964
Made public by his widow
Read in the House by Representative Charles A.
  Halleck of Indiana
Washington, D.C.
April 21, 1964

"We should not attempt to take over the war from the Vietnamese . . . no lasting solution can be imposed by foreign armies."

Hubert H. Humphrey
Senator from Minnesota
Washington, D.C.
September 12, 1964

"We have no plans at present to send combat troops to South Vietnam."

Robert S. McNamara
Secretary of Defense
Austin, Texas
November 10, 1964

"As you know, American troops have been sent to South Vietnam recently with the mission of protecting key installations there. In establishing and patrolling their defense perimeters, they come into contact with the Vietcong and at times are fired upon. Our troops naturally return the fire.

"It should come as no surprise, therefore, that our troops engage in combat in these and similar circumstances. But let me emphasize that the Vietnamese government forces are carrying the brunt of combat operations. Those United States forces assigned as advisors to the armed forces of Vietnam remain in that capacity."

Robert J. McCloskey
State Department press officer
Washington, D.C.
June 5, 1965

"American forces [will] be available for combat support together with Vietnamese forces when and if necessary . . . [as a] result of the best military judgment as to what is required in the situation ahead."

Robert J. McCloskey
State Department press officer
Washington, D.C.
June 8, 1965

"We have been moving in the direction of a massive, bog-down land struggle in Asia without any specific consent by Congress or the people for that kind of war."

Jacob K. Javits
Senator from New York
Washington, D.C.
June 9, 1965

"There has been no change in the mission of United States ground combat units in Vietnam in recent days or weeks . . . The primary mission of these troops is to secure and safeguard important military installations like the air base at Danang. They have the associated mission of active patrolling and securing action in and near the areas thus safeguarded.

"If help is requested by the appropriate Vietnamese commander, General Westmoreland also has the authority within the assigned mission to employ these troops in support of Vietnamese forces faced with aggressive attack when other effective reserves are not available and when, in his judgment, the general military situation requires it.

"This discretionary authority does not change the primary mission of United States troops in South Vietnam which has been approved by the President on advice and recommendation of responsible authorities.

"However, I would emphasize that any such change of primary mission would be a matter for decision in Washington."

White House statement
June 9, 1965

"I do not feel that the expanded use of American ground troops is an effective addition to the war."

Barry Goldwater
Former Senator from Arizona
Miami Beach, Florida
June 16, 1965

"The principal role of United States ground combat forces will be to supplement this reserve [of the South Vietnamese army] in support of the front-line forces of the South Vietnamese army."

Robert S. McNamara
Secretary of Defense
Washington, D.C.
August 4, 1965

"The commitment of American boys anywhere on the Asian mainland is a mistake."

Barry Goldwater
Former Senator from Arizona
Washington, D.C.
February 13, 1966

"I am convinced that the war effort will be served by a substantial increase in the Americans available on the ground and by a substantial increase in the air capability if American casualties and the casualties of South Vietnam and others engaged in this war are to be reduced."

Richard M. Nixon
Former Vice-President of the United States
Saigon, South Vietnam
August 7, 1966

"There is a grave danger at the present time that the administration will go overboard in increasing American forces in Vietnam. We might be able to win the war, but by doing so we would have on our hands a dependency for a long time to come. That's the wrong way to handle it."

Richard M. Nixon
Former Vice-President of the United States
Face the Nation (CBS-TV)
September 11, 1966

"I don't know how I might have decided it had I been in the White House at the time. I do remember reflecting at the time it happened that I thought President Kennedy did the right thing in approving the sending of 16,000 troops plus military advisors into the area."

Dwight D. Eisenhower
Former President of the United States
Indio, California
December 23, 1967

"By late spring of 1965 . . . it was my estimate that the government of [South] Vietnam could not survive . . . for more than six months unless the United States chose to increase its military commitment. Substantial numbers of U.S. ground combat forces were required."

General William C. Westmoreland
Chief of Staff, United States Army
Washington, D.C.
April 6, 1969

Why Are We There?

General

"Any move in Indo-China will be inspired by our desire to support and assist the national independence of Viet Nam."

Philip C. Jessup
United States Ambassador-at-Large
Jakarta, Indonesia
February 21, 1950

"What is it we are going to fight for and to defend? I am a Senator and I don't know. The Democratic Senators on the Armed Services and Foreign Relations Committees don't know."

Wayne Morse
Senator from Oregon
Washington, D.C.
April 5, 1954

"United States military and economic assistance and technical advice are being extended to the Republic of Vietnam at its request to assist the Vietnamese people to maintain their independence against this aggression . . .

"We have no combat units in that country and we have no desire for bases or other military advantages."

Dean Rusk
Secretary of State
Washington, D.C.
March 1, 1962

"I think our mission in Vietnam is very clear. We are there at the request of the South Vietnamese government to provide training."

Robert S. McNamara
Secretary of Defense
Washington, D.C.
March 15, 1962

"The principal objective of United States policy in Southeast Asia is simply to maintain the integrity and independence of the non-Communist nations in that area."

Robert S. McNamara
Secretary of Defense
Washington, D.C.
January 29, 1964

"The United States got into the guerrilla war in South Vietnam by mistake because Yo-Yo [Secretary of Defense Robert S. McNamara] went there and told these boys to start shooting when we were only supposed to be instructing."

Barry Goldwater
Senator from Arizona
Toledo, Ohio
September 30, 1964

"In 1954 two things were very clear: that in the absence of external help communism was virtually certain to take over the successor states of Indochina . . . and that with France no ready longer to act . . . no power other than the United States could move in to help fill the vacuum."

William P. Bundy
Assistant Secretary of State for Far Eastern Affairs
Washington, D.C.
January 23, 1965

"Our purpose in Vietnam is to join in the defense and protection of freedom of a brave people who are under attack that is controlled and that is directed from outside their country."

Lyndon B. Johnson
President of the United States
Washington, D.C.
February 17, 1965

"The people of South Vietnam have chosen to resist this threat. At their request, the United States has taken its place beside them in their defensive struggle."

"Aggression from the North"
State Department White Paper
February 27, 1965

"The fact that military hostilities have been taking place in Southeast Asia does not bring about the existence of a state of war, which is a legal characterization of a situation rather than a factual description. What we have in Viet-Nam is armed aggression from the North against the Republic of Viet-Nam. Pursuant to a South Vietnamese request and consultations between our

two Governments, South Viet-Nam and the
United States are engaged in collective defense
against that armed aggression. The inherent right
of individual and collective self-defense is recognized in article 51 of the United Nations Charter.

"If the question is intended to raise the issue of
legal authority to conduct the actions which have
been taken, there can be no doubt that these actions fall within the Constitutional powers of the
President and within the Congressional resolution of August 1964."

"Collective Defense Against Armed Aggression"
State Department White Paper
March 4, 1965

"We are there because we have a promise to keep."

Lyndon B. Johnson
President of the United States
Baltimore, Maryland
April 17, 1965

"The United States would never undertake the sacrifice these efforts require if its help were not wanted and requested."

Lyndon B. Johnson
President of the United States
Washington, D.C.
August 12, 1965

"We said we would help that country. We were not talking about military programs but foreign aid . . . there was no commitment given in a military context, except that as a part of SEATO."

Dwight D. Eisenhower
Former President of the United States
Washington, D.C.
August 17, 1965

"We are in Vietnam to safeguard the people, who are the real target of the enemy."

General Maxwell D. Taylor
Former United States Ambassador to South Vietnam
Washington, D.C.
February 17, 1966

"The more we Americanize the war . . . the more we make the war unwinable."

Arthur M. Schlesinger, Jr.
Former Presidential Assistant
Look Magazine
July 25, 1966

"I find that our effort is not appreciated.

"But what is more significant, it is not understood. If our aims were better understood, our effort would be more appreciated."

Richard M. Nixon
Former Vice-President of the United States
Paris, France
July 29, 1966

"The best way to make Communists is to put the Americans into a place where there were no Communists before."

Prince Norodom Sihanouk
Chief of State of Cambodia
Paris, France
February 24, 1967

"First, we were making the effort there so that people would have their own right to decide their own future, and could select their own form of government . . .

"Now we're saying we're going to fight there so that we don't have to fight in Thailand, so we don't have to fight on the West Coast of the United States, so that they won't move across the Rockies.

"Our whole moral position, it seems to me, changes tremendously."

Robert F. Kennedy
Senator from New York
Washington, D.C.
November 26, 1967

"The Americans are here to protect their interests, which do not always correspond with those of Vietnam. They are here because they want to remain in Asia to stop Communism in Asia—and not because they have any particular concern about us."

Nguyen Cao Ky
Vice-President of South Vietnam
Quoted in *Stern* Magazine
March 31, 1968

"I should state further that I certainly do not seek the Presidency for the purpose of presiding over the destruction of the credibility of American power throughout the world."

Richard M. Nixon
Former Vice-President of the United States
Miami Beach, Florida
August 6, 1968

"When we assumed the burden of helping defend South Vietnam, millions of South Vietnamese men, women and children placed their trust in us. To abandon them now would risk a massacre that would shock and dismay everyone in the world who values human life.

"Abandoning the South Vietnamese people, however, would jeopardize more than lives in South Vietnam. It would threaten our long-term hopes for peace in the world. A great nation cannot renege on its pledges. A great nation must be worthy of trust.

"If we simply abandoned our effort in Vietnam, the cause of peace might not survive the damage that would be done to other nations' confidence in our reliability."

Richard M. Nixon
President of the United States
Washington, D.C.
May 14, 1969

"It is shocking to realize that Congress was not asked for specific authority for the sending of American soldiers to South Vietnam and, indeed, that the government of South Vietnam itself did not make a written, formal request for these troops."

J. William Fulbright
Chairman of the Senate Foreign Relations Committee
Washington, D.C.
September 3, 1969

"The human, political and material costs of continuing our part in the war far outweigh any prospective benefits, and are greater than the foreseeable costs and risks of disengagement."

Daniel Ellsberg
Melvin Gurtov
Oleg Hoeffding
Arnold L. Horlick
Konrad Kellen
Paul F. Langer
Staff Members of the Rand Corporation, all of whom have done research on Vietnam for the Federal Government
Letter to the *New York Times* written as individuals and not in the capacity of Rand employees
October 8, 1969

"Everyone I have talked to [in Japan] says we have done our duty and met our commitment."

Hubert H. Humphrey
Former Vice-President of the United States
Tokyo, Japan
October 22, 1969

"We jumped into this area without knowing what we were jumping into."

Hubert H. Humphrey
Former Vice-President of the United States
Tokyo, Japan
October 22, 1969

"We are engaged in fighting a limited war, for limited objectives with limited resources. Our objective is not to win the war in the conventional sense. What we are aiming for is a negotiated settlement which will permit the people of South Vietnam to determine their own future."

Ellsworth Bunker
United States Ambassador to South Vietnam
Saigon, South Vietnam
January 29, 1970

"A just peace in Vietnam has been, and remains, our goal."

> Richard M. Nixon
> President of the United States
> Washington, D.C.
> February 18, 1970

"Why aren't we concerned with elections in Panama, Spain, Greece or Brazil?"

> J. William Fulbright
> Chairman of the Senate Foreign Relations Committee
> Washington, D.C.
> February 19, 1970

"The preservation of a non-Communist—as against a Communist—dictatorship in South Vietnam is not going to protect us, or anybody else, from Soviet or Chinese missiles."

> J. William Fulbright
> Chairman of the Senate Foreign Relations Committee
> Washington, D.C.
> April 2, 1970

"It simply does not matter very much for the United States, in cold, unadorned strategic terms, who rules the states of Indochina. Nor does it matter all that terribly much to the inhabitants. At the risk of being accused of every sin from racism to communism, I stress the irrelevance of ideology to poor and backward populations."

J. William Fulbright
Chairman of the Senate Foreign Relations Committee
Washington, D.C.
April 2, 1970

"It is tempting to take the easy political path . . . to get peace at any price now, even though I know that a peace of humiliation for the United States would lead to a bigger war or surrender later."

Richard M. Nixon
President of the United States
Washington, D.C.
April 30, 1970

"If when the chips are down, the world's most powerful nation—the United States of America —acts like a pitiful, helpless giant, the forces of totalitarianism and anarchy will threaten free nations and free institutions throughout the world."

Richard M. Nixon
President of the United States
Washington, D.C.
April 30, 1970

"I would rather be a one-term President and do what I believe was right than to be a two-term President at the cost of seeing America become a second-rate power and to see this nation accept the first defeat in its proud 190-year history."

Richard M. Nixon
President of the United States
Washington, D.C.
April 30, 1970

The Domino Theory

"Once Tongking [Northern Indo-China] is lost, there is really no barrier before Suez . . .

"The loss of Asia would mean the end of Islam, which has two thirds of its faithful in Asia. The fall of Islam would mean upheavals in North Africa jeopardizing the strategic European defense bases situated there."

General Jean de Lattre de Tassigny
Commander in Chief of French Forces in the Far East
Washington, D.C.
September 20, 1951

"The French are holding Indo-China, without which we would lose Japan and the Pacific."

Thomas E. Dewey
Governor of New York
Albany, N.Y.
February 19, 1952

"If Indo-China should be lost, there would be a chain reaction throughout the Far East and South Asia."

John Foster Dulles
Secretary of State
Washington, D.C.
May 5, 1953

"A grave threat to the Philippines, Australia and New Zealand."

John Foster Dulles
Secretary of State
Washington, D.C.
March 29, 1954

"A grave threat to Malaya, Thailand, Indonesia, the Philippines, Australia and New Zealand."

John Foster Dulles
Secretary of State
Washington, D.C.
April 5, 1954

"There was what you might call the 'falling domino' principle . . ."

Dwight D. Eisenhower
President of the United States
Washington, D.C.
April 6, 1954

"The loss of Indo-China would lead to the loss of Burma, Thailand, in fact, all of the great peninsula on which they are situated."

Dwight D. Eisenhower
President of the United States
Washington, D.C.
April 7, 1954

"What we are trying to do is create a situation in Southeast Asia where the Domino Theory will not apply."

John Foster Dulles
Secretary of State
Washington, D.C.
May 11, 1954

"On the fate of South Vietnam depends the fate of all of Asia. For South Vietnam is the dam in the river. A Communist victory there would mean, inevitably and soon, that the flood would begin; next would come the loss of Laos, Cambodia, Thailand, Malaysia and Indonesia, which is only forty-five miles from the Philippines and next door to Australia. Can anyone seriously suggest that in such a circumstance the United States would not have to engage in a major war to save the Philippines from the same fate as Vietnam? And what of Japan? . . .

"Overnight, the United States would cease to be a power on the world's greatest ocean. Our ships and planes could thereafter circumnavigate the globe only with Communist permission . . .

"Encouraged by our retreat the Communists will increase their aggressive action, not only in Asia, but in Africa, Latin America and the Near East."

Richard M. Nixon
Former Vice-President of the United States
Reader's Digest
August 1964

"If South Vietnam falls, the rest of Southeast
Asia will be in grave danger of progressively
disappearing behind the Bamboo Curtain, and
other Asian countries like India and even in time
Australia and your own [country] will in turn be
threatened."

William P. Bundy
Assistant Secretary of State for Far Eastern Affairs
Tokyo, Japan
September 29, 1964

"If Southeast Asia is allowed to fall, it will trigger
a big war to save the Philippines."

Richard M. Nixon
Former Vice-President of the United States
Salisbury, N.C.
October 10, 1964

"If we fail to draw the line in Vietnam we may
find ourselves compelled to draw a defense line as
far back as Seattle and Alaska, with Hawaii as a
solitary outpost in mid-Pacific."

Thomas J. Dodd
Senator from Connecticut
Washington, D.C.
February 23, 1965

"I have never believed in the simplicities of the domino theory . . .

"If you pressed me to say whether Indochina was vital to the security of the United States, I would have to say no. I don't think Vietnam is a testing place of American democracy or is strategically or otherwise important to United States interests.

"If we were not in Vietnam, all that part of the world would be enjoying the obscurity it so richly deserves."

John Kenneth Galbraith
Former United States Ambassador to India
Washington, D.C.
April 25, 1966

"They just keep trying to keep the people worried about the Communists crawling up the banks of Pearl Harbor, or crawling up the Palisades, or crawling up the beaches of Los Angeles, which of course is a bunch of pure, unadulterated poppycock.

"It's about eight thousand miles over the water, and as I said before, I don't think we have a record of but two people walking on water [Jesus and His disciple Peter], and one of them fell. They won't have enough ships in the next X years, or enough planes to get over. I don't know what they are going to get here with."

David M. Shoup
Former Commandant, U.S. Marine Corps
Washington, D.C.
December 18, 1967

"I never played dominoes, and I never took much stock in short labels to describe a complex situation until I felt that everybody knew what the label meant."

Dwight D. Eisenhower
Former President of the United States
Indio, California
December 23, 1967

SEATO

"Each party recognizes that aggression by means of armed attack would endanger its own peace and safety, and agrees that it will, in that event, act to meet the common danger in accordance with its constitutional processes."

SEATO Treaty
Article IV, Paragraph I
Signed by the United States on September 8, 1954

"The United States of America ought to mind its own business and keep out of foreign entanglements all over Europe and Asia. If there should be an uprising, all that would have to be done would be to charge such movements as being Communistic and immediately the United States would be called upon to take action."

William Langer
Senator from North Dakota
Voting against SEATO—Senate voted 82-1 in favor
Washington, D.C.
September 8, 1954

"The true measure of SEATO's worth is the simple fact that since we joined to create its protective shield there has been no Communist aggression against the treaty area."

C. Douglas Dillon
Under Secretary of State
Wellington, New Zealand
April 8, 1959

"We do believe that the obligations of the SEATO treaty are both joint and several, and that while the SEATO treaty is a substantiating basis for our presence there, we are not acting specifically under the SEATO treaty."

Dean Rusk
Secretary of State
Washington, D.C.
August 6, 1964

"The statement of the SEATO allies that Communist defeat is 'essential' is a reality. To fail to respond . . . would reflect on our honor as a nation, would undermine worldwide confidence in our courage, would convince every nation in Southeast Asia that it must bow to Communist terms to survive."

Lyndon B. Johnson
President of the United States
New York City
April 20, 1964

"It is this fundamental SEATO obligation that has, from the outset, guided our actions in Vietnam."

Dean Rusk
Secretary of State
Washington, D.C.
February 18, 1966

"We made those decisions [to intervene] because in the judgments of the Presidents [Kennedy and Johnson], American power and interests demanded it. Had the judgment been to the contrary, no treaty and no commitment would have forced us to the contrary.

"I have never heard a single person say to the President that we had to do this because of the [SEATO] treaty."

Richard N. Goodwin
Former speechwriter for Presidents Kennedy and
    Johnson
Washington, D.C.
February 4, 1967

Aggression from the North

"I think the pacification of the country would be easy if the external aggression were stopped."

Dean Rusk
Secretary of State
Washington, D.C.
February 25, 1965

"The record is conclusive. It establishes beyond question that North Viet-Nam is carrying out a carefully conceived plan of aggression against the South."

"Aggression from the North"
State Department White Paper
February 27, 1965

"There are elements of civil war in this situation, but the heart of the problem of peace is the external aggression."

Dean Rusk
Secretary of State
Washington, D.C.
February 18, 1966

"I think we are in there intervening in a civil war and our announced objectives are not attainable."

J. William Fulbright
Chairman of the Senate Foreign Relations Committee
Washington, D.C.
April 4, 1966

"I strongly resent the implication that the war in Vietnam is in any sense a civil war. It is the most flagrant case of outside aggression and intervention."

Robert S. McNamara
Secretary of Defense
Washington, D.C.
April 20, 1966

"It was the Americans who first intervened militarily in South Vietnam; it was only after the Americans came that North Vietnamese forces started going South. Now the United States is attacking the North. What would you expect the North Vietnamese to do?"

Prince Norodom Sihanouk
Chief of State of Cambodia
Pnompenh, Cambodia
September 4, 1966

"The United States now makes much of the action taken in Hanoi in 1956 to organize a liberation movement in the South, but how many people know that in 1956 Diem was promising to liberate the people of the North, meaning to unite Vietnam under his rule, and that in 1958, the Saigon government created the Committee for the Liberation of North Vietnam.

"By our standards that would be enough to justify Communist nations from all over the world to help North Vietnam put down an announced attempt on the part of the Saigon government to subvert North Vietnam in violation of the Geneva agreement."

Wayne Morse
Senator from Oregon
Granville, Ohio
December 4, 1966

"What we have is not civil war. It is a massive campaign of external aggression from North Vietnam."

General William C. Westmoreland
Commander, United States Forces in South Vietnam
New York City
April 24, 1967

"The U.S. combat forces did not go to South Vietnam because of the dissidence or the acts of violence of indigenous elements of the National Liberation Front. U.S. combat forces were injected because of the intrusion of North Vietnamese men, arms and regular units."

Dean Rusk
Secretary of State
Reader's Digest
December 1967

"What the Vietnam war amounts to is civil strife between those crooks in Saigon and Vietnamese nationals seeking a better life."

David M. Shoup
Former Commandant, U.S. Marine Corps
Washington, D.C.
December 18, 1967

4

Who's Winning?

1950 to the Geneva Agreements

"Viet Namese Premier Nguyen Phan Long promised today to defeat what the French say are Communist-led Nationalists in six months if his government got United States military and economic aid."

New York Times
February 15, 1950

"I do not think conditions in Indo-China are hopeless at all. They could become very good."

Robert Allen Griffin
Head of United States Aid Mission
Singapore
March 16, 1950

"American intervention in Indo-China is anti-democratic, bellicose, un-American, and certainly destined for the same fate as in China."

Ho Chi Minh
Leader of the Vietminh
Vietminh radio broadcast
August 4, 1950

"United States economic assistance is designed to stimulate conditions under which the people of Indo-China may develop institutions compatible with their religion and culture which will best serve the interests of the people."

Harry S. Truman
President of the United States
Washington, D.C.
August 13, 1950

"The war is costing France some billion dollars a year."

General Jean de Lattre de Tassigny
Commander in Chief of French Forces in the Far East
New York City
September 13, 1951

"With the assured support of as great a power as the United States, the people of Indo-China should get more of the confidence they badly need."

General Jean de Lattre de Tassigny
Commander in Chief of French Forces in the Far East
New York City
September 13, 1951

"There is no question that the Communist menace in French Indo-China has been stopped."

General J. Lawton Collins
Chief of Staff, United States Army
Taipei, Formosa
October 27, 1951

"The situation in Indo-China is better than last December and possibly the best since hostilities started."

Admiral Arthur W. Radford
Commander in Chief, United States Pacific Fleet
New Delhi, India
November 7, 1952

"With our new Vietnamese battalions, we think
we shall be able to clear the Red River delta by
1955."

General Raoul Salan
Commander of French Union Forces in Indochina
Saigon, Vietnam
March 6, 1953

"The progress already accomplished by the Associated States of Vietnam, Laos and Cambodia
in every field is remarkable and will not fail in the
long run to create a sure and solid barrier against
the onslaught of totalitarian Communism."

Donald R. Heath
United States Ambassador to Indochina
Paris, France
March 20, 1953

"There has been growing support among the thinking masses of the people of Cambodia to the theory that the Communist-led Vietminh is fighting for the independence of the country.

"They do not want to die for the French and help them stay here."

Prince Norodom Sihanouk
Chief of State of Cambodia
New York City
April 18, 1953

"We believe that the objectives of France, the United States and Vietnam are the same, that is, freedom and independence."

Richard M. Nixon
Vice-President of the United States
Saigon, South Vietnam
October 31, 1953

"We shall never abandon the Indo-Chinese peninsula to a foreign power."

Maurice Dejean
French Commissioner General
Hanoi, Vietnam
November 4, 1953

"We would all like to think the war there might be successfully concluded in the next calendar year."

John Foster Dulles
Secretary of State
Paris, France
December 14, 1953

"I do not believe that anything that has happened upsets appreciably the timetable of General Navarre's Plan [for the French to constantly maintain the initiative]. There is no reason that I am aware of for anybody to get panicky about what has happened."

John Foster Dulles
Secretary of State
Washington, D.C.
December 29, 1953

"I fully expect victory . . . after six more months of hard fighting."

General Henri-Eugene Navarre
Commander in Chief of French Forces
Hanoi, Vietnam
January 1, 1954

"It has been critical [in Indo-China] for so long that it is difficult to just point out a period when it is more than normally critical."

Dwight D. Eisenhower
President of the United States
Washington, D.C.
February 3, 1954

"The Navarre Plan is being successfully accomplished . . . later this year the victories should begin."

Malcolm MacDonald
British High Commissioner for Southeast Asia
Saigon, Vietnam
March 11, 1954

"If the Communists continue to suffer the losses they have been taking, I don't know how they can stay in the battle."

General Paul Ely
Chief of Staff of French Armed Forces
Washington, D.C.
March 20, 1954

"The French are going to win. It is a fight that is going to be finished with our help."

Admiral Arthur W. Radford
Chairman, Joint Chiefs of Staff
Washington, D.C.
March 22, 1954

"I do not expect that there is going to be a Communist victory in Indo-China.

"We have seen no reason to abandon the so-called Navarre Plan . . ."

John Foster Dulles
Secretary of State
Washington, D.C.
March 23, 1954

"The Navarre Plan is a plan designed by General Navarre to break the organized body of Communist aggression by the end of the 1955 fighting season and thereby reduce the fighting to guerrilla warfare which could, in 1956, be met for the most part by national forces of the three associated states Vietnam, Laos and Cambodia."

John Foster Dulles
Secretary of State
Washington, D.C.
April 5, 1954

"To pour money, matériel and men into the jungles of Indochina without at least a remote prospect of victory would be dangerously futile and self-destructive . . . I am frankly of the belief that no amount of American military assistance in Indochina can conquer an enemy which is everywhere and nowhere, 'an enemy of the people' which has the sympathy and covert support of the people."

John F. Kennedy
Senator from Massachusetts
Washington, D.C.
April 6, 1954

"There is no reason why the French forces should not remain in Indo-China and win. They have greater manpower, and a tremendous advantage over their adversaries, particularly air power."

Richard M. Nixon
Vice-President of the United States
Washington, D.C.
April 16, 1954

"There is no reason to question the inherent soundness of the Navarre Plan."

John Foster Dulles
Secretary of State
Washington, D.C.
April 6, 1954

"Our resistance is going to be overwhelmed. The Vietminh are now within a few meters from the radio transmitter where I am speaking."

Brigadier General Christian de Castries
French Commander at Dienbienphu
Dienbienphu, Vietnam
Last message before Vietminh take-over
May 7, 1954

"Dienbienphu has fulfilled the mission that was assigned to it by the high command."

Spokesman for General Henri-Eugene Navarre
Hanoi, Vietnam
After the fall of Dienbienphu
May 7, 1954

The Geneva Agreements to Tet 1968

"I still believe this country can be saved."

General John W. O'Daniel
Head of the United States Military Mission
Saigon, South Vietnam
December 16, 1954

"The situation is difficult but the present problems are neither unexpected nor insoluble."

John Foster Dulles
Secretary of State
Augusta, Georgia
April 17, 1955

"It is a strange and it is almost an inexplicable situation, at least from our viewpoint."

Dwight D. Eisenhower
President of the United States
Washington, D.C.
April 27, 1955

"Viet-Nam today, progressing rapidly to the establishment of democratic institutions by elective processes, its people resuming peaceful pursuits, its army growing in effectiveness, sense of mission and morale, the puppet Vietnamese politicians discredited, the refugees well on their way to permanent resettlement, the countryside generally orderly and calm, the predatory sects eliminated and their venal leaders exiled or destroyed."

Walter S. Robertson
Assistant Secretary of State for Far Eastern Affairs
Washington, D.C.
June 1, 1956

"South Vietnam is being turned into an American war base."

North Vietnamese protest to International Truce
   Control Commission in Vietnam
June 12, 1956

"For the first time in fifteen years Vietnam is enjoying full physical security. It is now possible for anyone to travel with assurance from Saigon and other populated areas to the remotest villages."

Nguyen Huu Hanh
Managing Director of the National Bank of South
    Vietnam
New York City
February 18, 1957

"The situation in South Vietnam is dangerous . . . there is still good reason for concern."

Admiral Harry D. Felt
Commander, United States Forces in the Pacific
Saigon, South Vietnam
September 28, 1961

"It is too late now to reverse the current against the West in Southeast Asia . . . Increased United States aid to Ngo Dinh Diem could only prolong the war in Vietnam . . . the result will be the same whether it is by negotiations or war, but the war will cost more in lives and dollars."

Prince Norodom Sihanouk
Chief of State of Cambodia
Pnompenh, Cambodia
November 16, 1961

"We are going to win in Vietnam. We will remain here until we do win."

Robert F. Kennedy
Attorney General
Saigon, Vietnam
February 18, 1962

"The French fought nine years in Vietnam and were kicked out. The Americans may fight fifteen years if they want to but it will not help."

Nikita Khrushchev
Premier of the U.S.S.R.
Sofia, Bulgaria
May 18, 1962

"The corner definitely has been turned toward victory in Vietnam."

Arthur Sylvester
Assistant Secretary of Defense
Washington, D.C.
May 7, 1963

"I feel that we shall achieve victory in 1964."

Tran Van Don
General in South Vietnamese Army
Ben Cat, South Vietnam
September 30, 1963

"I can safely say that the end of the war is in sight."

General Paul D. Harkins
United States Commander, South Vietnam
Tokyo, Japan
October 31, 1963

"We will stay for as long as it takes. We shall provide whatever help is required to win the battle against Communist insurgence."

Robert S. McNamara
Secretary of Defense
Saigon, South Vietnam
March 9, 1964

"I have already ordered measures to . . . keep our forces at whatever level continued independence and freedom require . . .

"Let no one doubt that we are in this battle as long as South Vietnam wants our support and needs our assistance."

Lyndon B. Johnson
President of the United States
New York City
April 20, 1964

"I don't think you can run this thing on a timetable and a schedule—we just make up our minds to stay with it as long as it takes."

Henry Cabot Lodge
Retiring United States Ambassador to South Vietnam
Saigon, South Vietnam
June 28, 1964

"There are a number of developments that make me think we are on the right track and that this effort is going to be successful."

Henry Cabot Lodge
Retiring United States Ambassador to South Vietnam
Saigon, South Vietnam
June 28. 1964

"Time and again we have demonstrated that we have no real intention of winning this war. Instead we are trying to achieve a precarious balance of not-quite-winning and not-quite-losing. Our allies in Asia are losing faith in us. Too often they have seen us falter and renege on our decisions."

Richard M. Nixon
Former Vice-President of the United States
Reader's Digest
August 1964

"Recently I undertook a journey through all of Southeast Asia. Every military man with whom I talked privately admitted that we are losing the war."

Richard M. Nixon
Former Vice-President of the United States
Reader's Digest
August 1964

"I think there may be some Americans who expect miracles from the United States in these far-off and distant places. Let me remind you once again that there are a billion and a half people in Asia . . . We are not going to find answers for a billion and a half people simply by saying to them, 'Now just move over and we Americans will settle these things for you.' That is not the way it's going to happen."

Dean Rusk
Secretary of State
Washington, D.C.
September 14, 1964

"We are fighting and losing Lyndon Johnson's war in Vietnam."

Barry Goldwater
Senator from Arizona
Dallas, Texas
September 23, 1964

"We are losing the war in Vietnam. If our strategy is not changed we will be thrown out in a matter of months—certainly within the year."

Richard M. Nixon
Former Vice-President of the United States
New York City
January 26, 1965

"It's a long, long way yet to go—three, four years."

Nguyen Cao Ky
Premier of South Vietnam
Washington, D.C.
July 19, 1965

"It will take two or three more years of intensive activity to win military victory over the Viet Cong."

Richard M. Nixon
Former Vice-President of the United States
Washington, D.C.
September 12, 1965

"We must never forget that if the war in Vietnam is lost . . . the right of free speech will be extinguished throughout the world."

Richard M. Nixon
Former Vice-President of the United States
New York City
October 27, 1965

"The tide of battle has turned."

Hubert H. Humphrey
Vice-President of the United States
Washington, D.C.
February 24, 1966

"This is and was the wrong place to make a stand. I don't think we can roll back the area controlled by the Vietcong for ten years and I question the wisdom of investing the lives of other peoples in trying."

John Kenneth Galbraith
Former United States Ambassador to India
Washington, D.C.
April 25, 1966

82

"It appears that the Vietcong is losing what support it had from the rural population."

Robert S. McNamara
Secretary of Defense
Washington, D.C.
May 11, 1966

"In two or three years, or even before, the Communists will accept defeat."

Nguyen Cao Ky
Premier of South Vietnam
Saigon, South Vietnam
August 13, 1966

"A Communist take-over is no longer just improbable; as long as the United States and our brave allies are in the field, it is impossible."

Lyndon B. Johnson
President of the United States
Johnson City, Texas
August 14, 1966

"We are in a much stronger position than two years ago . . . They will not be able to succeed here."

Dean Rusk
Secretary of State
Saigon, South Vietnam
December 9, 1966

"We've reached a point where all the king's horses and all the king's men are not going to move us out of our position."

Lyndon B. Johnson
President of the United States
Washington, D.C.
February 20, 1967

"It can be said now that the defeat of the Communist forces in South Vietnam is inevitable. The only question is, how soon?"

Richard M. Nixon
Former Vice-President of the United States
Saigon, South Vietnam
April 17, 1967

"Two years ago South Vietnam was on the verge of defeat."

General William C. Westmoreland
Commander, United States Forces in South Vietnam
New York City
April 24, 1967

"The military picture is favorable."

General William C. Westmoreland
Commander, United States Forces in South Vietnam
New York City
April 24, 1967

"The war is not a stalemate. We are winning it slowly but steadily. North Vietnam is paying a tremendous price with nothing to show for it in return."

General William C. Westmoreland
Commander, United States Forces in South Vietnam
Saigon, South Vietnam
July 7, 1967

"I believe we are gradually achieving our aims in Vietnam."

Ellsworth Bunker
United States Ambassador to South Vietnam
Saigon, South Vietnam
July 8, 1967

"Some more troops will be needed."

Robert S. McNamara
Secretary of Defense
Washington, D.C.
July 12, 1967

"We have made steady progress for the last two years, and especially in the last six months."

General William C. Westmoreland
Commander, United States Forces in South Vietnam
Saigon, South Vietnam
July 23, 1967

"I have never been more encouraged in my four years in Vietnam."

General William C. Westmoreland
Commander, United States Forces in South Vietnam
Washington, D.C.
November 15, 1967

86

"We are at the point now not only of being able to continue, but to accelerate the rate of progress."

Ellsworth Bunker
United States Ambassador to South Vietnam
Washington, D.C.
November 19, 1967

"We are winning . . . It is pretty obvious that about all the enemy can do is resort to guerrilla tactics in large parts of the country and wait for an opportunity to take on our big units near his border sanctuaries."

Admiral U.S. Grant Sharp
Commander, United States Forces in the Pacific
Honolulu, Hawaii
November 21, 1967

"Through careful exploitation of the enemy's vulnerability and application of our superior fire power and mobility we should expect our gains of 1967 to be increased manyfold in 1968 . . .

"Our forces have been able to detect impending major offensives and to mount spoiling attacks."

General William C. Westmoreland
Commander, United States Forces in South Vietnam
Saigon, South Vietnam
January 1, 1968

"Eleven and a half million people of South Vietnam's seventeen and a half million population now live in secure or reasonably secure areas."

Robert W. Komer
Civilian Administrator of American Pacification
  Program
Saigon, South Vietnam
January 24, 1968

"This situation is getting more serious with Communist attacks against seven province capitals in Central Vietnam and the highlands on the very night of the [lunar] New Year [Tet]. The general offensive scheme of the Communists was most conspicuous last night when they infiltrated into Saigon with the purpose of occupying or destroying a number of government offices and attacked other province capitals in the Mekong River delta . . .

"[Therefore,] I declare the state of martial law throughout the nation from today until further notice."

Nguyen Van Thieu
President of South Vietnam
Saigon, South Vietnam
January 31, 1968

"In my opinion this is a diversionary effort to take attention away from the northern part of the country."

General William C. Westmoreland
Commander, United States Forces in South Vietnam
Saigon, South Vietnam
February 1, 1968

"We have known for some time that this offensive was planned by the enemy . . . The ability to do what they have done has been anticipated, prepared for, and met.

"The stated purposes of the general uprising have failed . . . as a military movement it has been a failure . . . I do not believe that they wlll achieve a psychological victory."

Lyndon B. Johnson
President of the United States
Washington, D.C.
February 2, 1968

"If taking over a section of the American Embassy, a good part of Hue, Dalat and major cities of the Fourth Corps area constitutes complete failure, I suppose by this logic that if the Vietcong capture the entire country, the administration would be claiming their total collapse."

Eugene J. McCarthy
Senator from Minnesota
Washington, D.C.
February 3, 1968

"There is no question but that the peoples of the cities and the towns of South Vietnam have been dealt a heavy blow. They must have been surprised and impressed by the weight of the attack."

Robert S. McNamara
Secretary of Defense
Washington, D.C.
February 4, 1968

"I don't want any damned Dienbienphu."

Lyndon B. Johnson
President of the United States
Washington, D.C.
February 4, 1968

"It became necessary to destroy the town to save it."

Unnamed Major in the United States Army
Bentre, South Vietnam (population, 35,000)
February 7, 1968

"Half a million American soldiers, with 700,000 Vietnamese allies, with total command of the air, total command of the sea, backed by huge resources and the most modern weapons, are unable to secure even a single city from the attacks of an enemy whose total strength is about 250,000."

Robert F. Kennedy
Senator from New York
Washington, D.C.
February 8, 1968

"The time has come for us to realize that we have lost this war in terms of what was our original objective. We've proved to ourselves and everyone else that we'd be very reluctant to get in a similar situation."

Edwin O. Reischauer
Former United States Ambassador to Japan
Washington, D.C.
February 11, 1968

After Tet 1968

"I do not believe Hanoi can hold up under a long war."

General William C. Westmoreland
Commander, United States Forces in South Vietnam
Saigon, South Vietnam
February 25, 1968

"Militarily we have never been in a better relative position in South Vietnam."

General William C. Westmoreland
Commander, United States Forces in South Vietnam
Washington, D.C.
April 7, 1968

"The enemy has been defeated at every turn."

General William C. Westmoreland
Commander, United States Forces in South Vietnam
Saigon, South Vietnam
June 9, 1968

94

"Some United States units in Vietnam really count bodies. Others probably never do, but under pressure from higher up, report whatever body count would be expected for a particular action . . .

"[We are in danger] of falling victim to our own inflated statistics . . . [plans] based on exaggerated enemy casualties can result in disaster . . .

"[When] even high-speed aircraft flying over jungle terrain began reporting body counts of their own, the credibility of the term became quickly strained."

Lieutenant Colonel Richard A. McMahon
Army intelligence officer who served in South Vietnam
Washington, D.C.
June 28, 1968

"It has been evident from witnesses that it did not dawn on our top leaders that the Tet offensive was going to happen when it did."

Jamie L. Whitten
Member of House Appropriations Subcommittee
Washington, D.C.
July 9, 1968

"Our forces have achieved an unbroken string of victories which, in the aggregate, is something new in our military history."

General Earle G. Wheeler
Chairman, Joint Chiefs of Staff
Washington, D.C.
August 31, 1968

"There is growing hope for an end to this war, perhaps sooner than many yet dare to think."

Robert W. Komer
Civilian Administrator of American Pacification
    Program
Saigon, South Vietnam
September 23, 1968

"I would say quite definitely at this moment that the South Vietnamese and the Americans have the upper hand on the military side."

Sir Robert Thompson
Special Advisor to President Richard M. Nixon
London, England
December 14, 1969

96

"To date the pacification program is succeeding."

Richard M. Nixon
President of the United States
Washington, D.C.
February 18, 1970

"We finally have in sight the just peace we are seeking."

Richard M. Nixon
President of the United States
San Clemente, California
April 20, 1970

"After consulting with his commanders ten days ago, he [President Nixon] could announce withdrawal of 150,000 troops and express confidence a just peace was in sight, whereas tonight he said this action [attacking enemy sanctuaries in Cambodia] was indispensable to the withdrawal of those troops. He was either wrong ten days ago or he is wrong now."

Edmund S. Muskie
Senator from Maine
Washington, D.C.
April 30, 1970

"They have been in a war for years and years and they are quite debilitated and decimated, and I don't think they are capable with any kind of resistance of continuing this fight."

Spiro T. Agnew
Vice-President of the United States
Face the Nation (CBS-TV)
May 3, 1970

The Vice-President: "You would admit, I believe, that there has been a great diminution in their [the North Vietnamese] capability and in their activity in recent years."

Reporter: "You mean light at the end of the tunnel?"

The Vice-President: "Yes, exactly."

Spiro T. Agnew
Vice-President of the United States
Face the Nation (CBS-TV)
May 3, 1970

5

The Tonkin Incident

"While on routine patrol in international waters . . . the United States destroyer *Maddox* underwent an unprovoked attack by three PT-type boats . . . in Tonkin Gulf.

"The PT boats were driven off, with one seen to be badly damaged and not moving and the other two damaged and retreating slowly. No casualties or damage was sustained by the *Maddox*."

Defense Department statement
Washington, D.C.
August 2, 1964

"The other side got a sting out of this [the Tonkin Gulf incident involving the *Maddox*]. If they do it again they'll get another sting."

Dean Rusk
Secretary of State
Washington, D.C.
August 2, 1964

"A second deliberate attack was made during darkness by an undetermined number of North Vietnamese PT boats on the USS *Maddox* and the USS *C. Turner Joy* . . .

"The attackers were driven off, with no United States casualties, no hits and no damage to either destroyer.

"It is believed that at least two of the PT boats were sunk and two others damaged."

Pentagon statement
Washington, D.C.
August 4, 1964

"As I speak to you tonight, air action is now in execution against gunboats and certain supporting facilities in North Vietnam which have been used in these hostile actions."

Lyndon B. Johnson
President of the United States
Washington, D.C.
August 4, 1964

"Our vessels when attacked were operating . . .
roughly sixty miles off of the North Vietnamese
coast."

Robert S. McNamara
Secretary of Defense
Washington, D.C.
August 5, 1964

"A sheer fabrication."

Radio Hanoi
Reply to United States announcement of second
attack by North Vietnamese PT boats on American
destroyers
August 5, 1964

"The *Maddox* began shooting at North Vietnamese PT boats because she believed she was
going to be attacked. But that is not the same as
being attacked."

Wayne Morse
Senator from Oregon
Los Angeles, California
August 29, 1964

"The ships had great difficulty in determining
what was happening because they were operating
in darkness."

Robert S. McNamara
Secretary of Defense
Washington, D.C.
October 6, 1964

"Any suggestion that the August 1964 attacks on
United States destroyers in the Tonkin Gulf did
not occur is contrary to known facts."

Defense Department statement
Washington, D.C.
December 22, 1967

"The punitive air strikes immediately following
the Tonkin Gulf incident in late 1964 revealed the
readiness of naval air forces to bomb North Vietnam. It now appears that the Navy actually had
attack plans ready even before the alleged incident took place!"

David M. Shoup
Former Commandant, U.S. Marine Corps
Atlantic Magazine
April, 1969

6

The Tonkin Resolution

"I shall immediately request the Congress to pass
a resolution making it clear that our government
is united in its determination to take all necessary
measures in support of freedom and in defense of
peace in Southeast Asia.

"I have been given encouraging assurance by
these leaders of both parties that such a resolution will be promptly introduced, freely and ex-
peditiously debated, and passed with over-
whelming support."

Lyndon B. Johnson
President of the United States
Washington, D.C.
August 4, 1964

"Whereas naval units of the Communist regime in Viet-Nam, in violation of the Charter of the United Nations and of international law, have deliberately and repeatedly attacked U.S. naval vessels lawfully present in international waters, and have thereby created a serious threat to international peace;

"Whereas these attacks are part of a deliberate and systematic campaign of aggression that the Communist regime in North Viet-Nam has been waging against its neighbors and the nations joined with them in the collective defense of their freedom;

"Whereas the United States is assisting the peoples of Southeast Asia to protect their freedom and has no territorial, military or political ambitions in that area but desires only that they should be left in peace to work out their own destinies in their own way: Now, therefore, be it

"Resolved by the Senate and House of Representatives of the United States of America in Congress assembled, that the Congress approves and supports the determination of the President, as Commander-in-Chief, to take all necessary measures to repel any armed attack against the forces of the United States and to prevent further aggression."

Public Law 86-408
"The Tonkin Resolution"
Approved August 10, 1964

"Our continuing policy is to limit our role to the provision of aid, training assistance and military advice, and it is the sense of Congress that, except when provoked to a greater response, we should continue to attempt to avoid a direct military involvement in the Southeast Asian conflict."

Amendment proposed to The Tonkin Resolution by
   Senator Gaylord Nelson of Wisconsin
August 7, 1964

[The above was not added to the resolution because it would have caused a proceedural delay, but was pronounced:]

   "Unobjectionable . . . an accurate reflection of what I believe is the President's policy."

J. William Fulbright
Senate floor manager of "The Tonkin Resolution"
Washington, D.C.
August 7, 1964

"That language, just as a reminder to you, said: 'The Congress approves and supports the determination of the President as Commander-in-Chief to take all—all—all necessary measures to repel any—any—any armed attack against the forces of the United States.' "

Lyndon B. Johnson
President of the United States
Washington, D.C.
June 17, 1965

"Any time they [Congress] want to take the authority the [Tonkin] resolution gives me, they can just take it away."

Lyndon B. Johnson
President of the United States
Washington, D.C.
June 17, 1965

"I continue to be guided in these matters by the resolution of the Congress approved on August 10, 1964—Public Law 86-408—by a vote of 504 to 2."

Lyndon B. Johnson
President of the United States
Washington, D.C.
January 28, 1966

"That resolution was drafted by the executive and sent up here. We didn't draft it, but we did, under the impeller of the emergency, accept it . . . largely without any consideration."

J. William Fulbright
Chairman of the Senate Foreign Relations Committee
Washington, D.C.
August 17, 1967

"Didn't that resolution authorize the President to use the armed forces of the United States in whatever way was necessary? Didn't it? What could a declaration of war have done that would have given the President more authority and a clearer voice of the Congress than that did?"

Nicholas deB. Katzenbach
Under Secretary of State
Washington, D.C.
August 17, 1967

"I did not vote for the resolution with any understanding that it was tantamount to a declaration of war."

Albert Gore
Senator from Tennessee
Washington, D.C.
August 17, 1967

7

Bombing

"The basic objective of the strikes has been to inhibit, to reduce, to deflect, the movement southward of men and matériel."

Robert S. McNamara
Secretary of Defense
Washington, D.C.
April 26, 1965

"It is my opinion that the bombings [of North Vietnam] will not have much effect one way or the other. I don't think we will gain much by it or lose much."

Richard B. Russell
Senator from Georgia
Washington, D.C.
May 5, 1965

"To increase the bombing and to bomb Hanoi—
or even Peking—will add to our problems rather
than detract from them, and it will not stop the
penetrations of North Vietnam troops into the
South."

James M. Gavin
Former General, United States Army
Harper's Magazine
February 1966

"I would doubt if we would find many of the
bombs hitting exactly where we would like them
to go simply because of the fact this is area bombing, and, as I say, based on generalized intelligence; but the over-all effect has been very
helpful."

General Maxwell D. Taylor
Former United States Ambassador to South Vietnam
Washington, D.C.
February 17, 1966

"In spite of their defiant statements of determination to endure these attacks forever, I for one know from experience that no one derives any enjoyment from receiving incoming shells and bombs day after day."

General Maxwell D. Taylor
Former United States Ambassador to South Vietnam
Washington, D.C.
February 17, 1966

"Officialdom in Washington has brainwashed itself to the extent that Chinese air bases are called 'sanctuaries' just as though they had no right to fly thirty miles across their border over North Vietnam, but we have every right to fly thousands of miles from our border to bomb North Vietnam."

Wayne Morse
Senator from Oregon
Portland, Oregon
April 30, 1966

"This bombing program to the North . . . is supplemental to the battle in the South."

General William C. Westmoreland
Commander, United States Forces in South Vietnam
Johnson City, Texas
August 14, 1966

"I don't believe that any amount of bombing, within practical limits, of North Vietnam would have substantially reduced . . . infiltration."

Robert S. McNamara
Secretary of Defense
Washington, D.C.
January 1967

"You've got to forget about this civilian stuff. Whenever you drop bombs you're going to hit civilians; it's foolish to pretend you're not."

Barry Goldwater
Former Senator from Arizona
New York City
January 23, 1967

"I want to say categorically that it is not the position of the American government that the bombing will be decisive in getting Hanoi to abandon aggression."

Lyndon B. Johnson
President of the United States
Nashville, Tennessee
March 16, 1967

"We must be willing to continue our bombing until we have destroyed every work of man in North Vietnam if this is what it takes to win the war."

Curtis LeMay
Former General, U.S. Air Force
Long Beach, California
April 1, 1967

"There were times when pilots would bomb the same railroad car fifteen times during the month. Each time the bomb assessment was 'target destroyed.'

"Flight after flight dropped bombs on targets that had been hit over and over again."

Alex Waier
Former Navy A-1 Skyraider pilot
Midland, Michigan
August 15, 1967

"North Vietnam had no real war-making industrial base and hence none which could be destroyed by bombing . . .

"There is no basis to believe that any bombing campaign, short of one that had population as its target, would itself force Ho Chi Minh's regime into submission . . .

"There are only fifty-seven targets recommended by the Joint Chiefs of Staff against which strikes have not yet been authorized. Whatever the merits of striking these fifty-seven targets may be, I believe that it is clear that strikes against them will not materially shorten the war. As a matter of fact, seven of the fifty-seven targets are recognized by the Chiefs as of little value to the North Vietnamese war effort. For example, one is a tire plant reported to have a productive capacity of but thirty tires per day. Nine of the fifty-seven targets are petroleum facilities which in total equal less than six percent of North Vietnam's remaining storage capacity. The present importance of such targets as these has not been shown to warrant risking the loss of American lives . . .

"The total number of fixed targets struck in North Vietnam stands now at 1,900 . . . decisions to authorize new targets cannot be expected to gain different objectives than those toward which our air campaign has always been directed . . .

"Enemy operations in the South cannot, on the basis of reports I have seen, be stopped by air bombardment . . .

"Bombing the ports and mining the harbors would not be an effective means of stopping the infiltration of supplies into South Vietnam."

Robert S. McNamara
Secretary of Defense
Washington, D.C.
August 25, 1967

"The subcommittee has always recognized that the air war in the North is not a substitute for the ground war in South Vietnam."

Senate Preparedness Investigation Subcommittee
   report
Washington, D.C.
August 31, 1967

"They don't bomb us, so they can't talk about 'we won't bomb you if you don't bomb us.' We will continue to supply our troops at the front [during the bombing pause] so they will continue to supply theirs. Yet we expect them not to, I presume, as a reciprocal act."

James M. Gavin
Former General, United States Army
Washington, D.C.
November 12, 1967

"We have dropped twelve tons of bombs for every square mile of North and South Vietnam. Whole provinces have been substantially destroyed. More than two million South Vietnamese are now homeless refugees."

Robert F. Kennedy
Senator from New York
Washington, D.C.
February 8, 1968

[Marines stationed around the demilitarized zone have suffered] "no adverse effects because of the bombing halt yet."

General Leonard F. Chapman, Jr.
Commandant, U.S. Marine Corps
Tokyo, Japan
January 6, 1969

"It became increasingly apparent that the U.S. bombing effort in both North and South Vietnam has been one of the most wasteful and expensive hoaxes ever to be put over on the American people."

David M. Shoup
Former Commandant, U.S. Marine Corps
Atlantic Magazine
April 1969

"It is my opinion that if we had continued to bomb [North Vietnam], the war would be over at this time—or would be nearly over."

> General William C. Westmoreland
> Army Chief of Staff
> Washington, D.C.
> December 1, 1969

"It [renewed bombing of North Vietnamese targets] is not a new policy at all. We have before on previous occasions made these attacks when it was necessary to protect reconnaissance flights, part of the arrangement made with North Vietnam when we stopped the bombing."

> William P. Rogers
> Secretary of State
> Washington, D.C.
> May 1, 1970

"The attacks in North Vietnam, just across the DMZ, have traditionally been ones of what we call 'protective reaction.'"

> Spiro T. Agnew
> Vice-President of the United States
> *Face the Nation* (CBS-TV)
> May 3, 1970

"We Seek No Wider War"

"The United States . . . seeks no wider war."
Lyndon B. Johnson
President of the United States
Washington, D.C.
June 23, 1964

"The administration plans to prepare to move into North Vietnam."
Melvin R. Laird
Representative from Wisconsin
Washington, D.C.
May 31, 1964

"We are going to drive the Communists out of South Vietnam even if that eventually involves a choice of attacking countries to the north.

"If Communist forces get the upper hand in Laos, the only response we would have would be to put our own forces in there."

William P. Bundy
Assistant Secretary of State
Washington, D.C.
June 18, 1964

"Air action is now in execution against gunboats and certain supporting facilities in North Vietnam which have been used in these hostile operations.

"We . . . seek no wider war."

Lyndon B. Johnson
President of the United States
Washington, D.C.
August 4, 1964

"I have had advice to load our planes with bombs and to drop them on certain areas that I think would enlarge the war and escalate the war, and result in committing a good many American boys to fighting a war that I think ought to be fought by the boys of Asia to help protect their own land. And for that reason I haven't chosen to enlarge the war."

Lyndon B. Johnson
President of the United States
Stonewall, Texas
August 29, 1964

"We can plainly say we are not escalating the war."

John A. Sparkman
Senator from Alabama
Washington, D.C.
January 15, 1965

"We seek no wider war."

William P. Bundy
Assistant Secretary of State for Far Eastern Affairs
Washington, D.C.
January 23, 1965

"We seek no wider war."

White House announcement of air strikes on North
  Vietnam
Washington, D.C.
February 7, 1965

"On February 11 United States air elements joined with the South Vietnamese air force in attacks against military facilities in North Vietnam used by Hanoi for the training and infiltrating of Vietcong into South Vietnam.

"These actions by the South Vietnamese and United States governments were in response to further direct provocations by the Hanoi regime.

"While maintaining their desire to avoid spreading the conflict, the two governments felt compelled to take the action described above."

White House announcement of air strikes on North Vietnam
Washington, D.C.
February 12, 1965

"The United States still seeks no wider war."

Lyndon B. Johnson
President of the United States
Washington, D.C.
March 25, 1965

"We still seek no wider war."

Lyndon B. Johnson
President of the United States
Washington, D.C.
April 25, 1965

"I have asked the commanding general, General Westmoreland, what more he needs to meet this mounting aggression. He has told me. And we will meet his needs . . .

"We do not want an expanding struggle with consequences that no one can foresee, nor will we bluster or bully or flaunt our power. But we will not surrender and we will not retreat."

Lyndon B. Johnson
President of the United States
Washington, D.C.
July 28, 1965

"The United States could not win militarily in a classic sense—because of our national policy of not expanding the war."

General William C. Westmoreland
Commander, United States Forces in South Vietnam
Saigon, South Vietnam
June 10, 1968

"U.S. aircraft conduct limited reconnaissance flights over North Vietnam. These flights do not involve the use of force and pose no threat to the security of North Vietnam but are essential for the security and safety of allied forces in South Vietnam.

"These flights are in keeping with the understanding reached at the time of the cessation of bombing of North Vietnam. When North Vietnamese forces attack these reconnaissance planes, necessary measures are taken in self-defense. Consequently, the Democratic Republic of Vietnam must bear full responsibility for incidents caused by its action against such planes."

Philip C. Habib
Acting Head of the United States Delegation to the
  Paris Peace Talks
Paris, France
January 29, 1970

"The U.S. Command has previously said that
when fired upon from enemy positions outside
the Republic of Vietnam, U.S. forces are authorized to return fire. This is an inherent right of
self-defense against enemy attacks."

Statement issued by United States Command in South
  Vietnam
Saigon, South Vietnam
February 11, 1970

"In cooperation with the armed forces of South
Vietnam, attacks are being launched this week to
clean out major enemy sanctuaries on the Cam-
bodian-Vietnam border . . .

   "We shall avoid a wider war . . ."

Richard M. Nixon
President of the United States
Washington, D.C.
April 30, 1970

When Will They Attack Again?

"We expect another major offensive, against Saigon and elsewhere, sometime in August or September."

Unnamed General in United States Army
Saigon, South Vietnam
July 16, 1968

"We had an offensive over Tet and a series of significant attacks in May. It is anticipated that there will be other attacks of this kind in July and August."

Clark M. Clifford
Secretary of Defense
Danang, South Vietnam
July 17, 1968

"We have much information that they are building up supplies for an attack in the next two or three months."

Lieutenant General Hoang Xuam Lam
Commander of South Vietnamese Troops in I Corps
Danang, South Vietnam
July 26, 1968

"The enemy is preparing a massive attack on our forces and those of our allies."

Lyndon B. Johnson
President of the United States
Washington, D.C.
July 31, 1968

"In the middle of June a military spokesman cautioned that June 20 was the target date . . . 'They called that one off,' a high-ranking officer explained . . . A month later reporters were called to a briefing at which it was said that July 20 would be a time of terrorist attacks throughout Saigon and the country."

Douglas Robinson
New York Times
Saigon, South Vietnam
August 1, 1968

126

"We're sure they're planning something. Too many prisoners have told us about it for us to think it is a deception, but, of course, we can never be sure they will not call it off."

Unnamed American military official
Saigon, South Vietnam
August 6, 1968

"The Vietcong intend to strike again on September 2."

Nguyen Van Thieu
President of South Vietnam
Saigon, South Vietnam
August 21, 1968

"Intelligence officers have been speculating for days that the enemy would attempt a coordinated thrust against the allies sometime after mid-December."

Joseph B. Treaster
New York Times
Saigon, South Vietnam
December 12, 1968

"We have intelligence reports that the Communists will try to attack us on Tet [February 17]."
    Civilian spokesman for the Saigon Government
    Saigon, South Vietnam
    February 16, 1969

"There are good intelligence indications that the enemy plans new offensive actions this spring or summer."
    Ellsworth Bunker
    United States Ambassador to South Vietnam
    Saigon, South Vietnam
    January 29, 1970

10

The Geneva Agreements

"The United States will not sign an Indo-China settlement, but will not do anything to upset any reasonable accord sought by France."

John Foster Dulles
Secretary of State
Washington, D.C.
July 19, 1954

Chapter II Article 14 Section a: Pending the general elections which will bring about the unification of Viet-Nam, the conduct of civil administration in each regrouping zone shall be in the hands of the party whose forces are to be regrouped there in virtue of the present Agreement.

Chapter III Article 16: The introduction into Viet-Nam of any troop reinforcements and additional military personnel is prohibited.

Agreement on the Cessation of Hostilities in
  Viet-Nam, July 20, 1954

5.   No military base under the control of a foreign state may be established in the regrouping
zones of the two parties.
7.   In order to ensure that sufficient progress in
the restoration of peace has been made, and that
all the necessary conditions obtain for free ex-
pression of the national will, general elections
shall be held in July 1956.

Final Declaration of Geneva Conference,
July 21, 1954

"United States ruling circles show a deliberate
desire to deepen their intervention in the internal
affairs of Vietnam to prevent the implementation
of the Geneva Agreements and to prepare for a
definitive partition of Vietnam."

Pham Van Dong
Foreign Minister of North Vietnam
Hanoi, North Vietnam
December 8, 1954

"North Vietnam seeks consultations on free general elections throughout the whole territory of Vietnam with guarantees of freedom of electioneering for all political parties, organizations and individuals."

Pham Van Dong
Deputy Premier of North Vietnam
Hanoi, North Vietnam
June 6, 1955

"We do not consider ourselves bound by the Geneva Agreement, which has been signed against the will and in contempt of the interest of the Vietnamese people."

South Vietnam National Assembly
Saigon, South Vietnam
March 8, 1956

"Efforts to unify Vietnam are constantly hampered by American imperialism and its puppets from South Vietnam."

Ho Chi Minh
President of North Vietnam
Belgrade, Yugoslavia
August 5, 1957

"We seek the full and effective restoration of the international agreements signed in Geneva in 1954, with respect to South Vietnam."

Lyndon B. Johnson
President of the United States
Washington, D.C.
August 5, 1964

"We seek no more than a return to the essentials of the agreements of 1954."

Lyndon B. Johnson
President of the United States
Washington, D.C.
March 25, 1965

"The Geneva negotiations were conducted by me in close and continuous cooperation with the United States delegation and particularly with its head, General [Walter] Bedell-Smith, who approved and supported, day after day, the efforts pursued by Mr. Anthony Eden [then Prime Minister of Great Britain] and myself.

"The conditions finally stipulated at Geneva were, in the end, better that the 'seven points' of June 28, 1954, formulated at the Washington meeting of John Foster Dulles and Anthony Eden.

"President Eisenhower, stating that the Geneva Agreements had made 'the best of a bad bargain,' further declared on July 21, 1954, that there was 'no visable alternative' and therefore he was not going to criticize what others did."

Pierre Mendés-France
Former Premier of France
Boston, Massachusetts
February 18, 1966

11

"The Legal Government of Vietnam"

"We are behind the legal government of Vietnam."

General J. Lawton Collins
Special United States Ambassador to South Vietnam
Washington, D.C.
April 21, 1955

"In him [Diem] his country has found a truly worthy leader whose integrity and devotion to his country's welfare have become generally recognized among his people. Asia has given us in President Diem another great figure, and the entire free world has become the richer for his example of determination and moral fortitude.

"The United States is proud to be on the side of the effort of the Vietnamese people under President Diem to establish freedom, peace and the good life."

Walter S. Robertson
Assistant Secretary of State for Far Eastern Affairs
Washington, D.C.
June 1, 1956

"I do not exaggerate when I say that your friends everywhere have derived great inspiration from the successes which have marked the first two years of President Ngo Dinh Diem's administration."

Richard M. Nixon
Vice-President of the United States
Saigon, South Vietnam
July 6, 1956

"President Ngo Dinh Diem, a man history may yet judge as one of the great figures of the twentieth century."

> Robert Wagner
> Mayor of New York City
> New York City
> May 13, 1957

"We follow the same line as the President [Diem] with this difference, that we would like to have a regime without corruption—with more liberty and efficiency . . . The President's policies have only oppressed the people, not protected them from Communists."

> Petition signed by eighteen well-known South
>   Vietnamese asking for an end to dictatorial rule
> Saigon, South Vietnam
> April 30, 1960

"In my opinion, to win this war we must show the people the difference between Communism and democracy. The population of South Vietnam sees that the policy of Mr. Diem is exactly like that of the Communists—if not worse. In South Vietnam there are the concentration camps, the false elections and the political control of the army and the complete control of the people just as in a Communist country. And in addition, there is the terrible corruption at all levels of the Diem regime.

"The United States will not engage in a long, undeclared war against Communism in South Vietnam—public opinion at home would not permit it once the American people see that it cannot be won and that in any case there are no differences between the Diem regime and Communism."

Lieutenant Colonel Vuong Van Dong
Leader of unsuccessful coup against Diem in
    November 1960
Pnompenh, Cambodia
July 10, 1962

"The question of how much popular support Diem enjoys should be considered in terms of how much popular support his opponents command. Neither of the recent non-Communist attempts to overthrow him appeared to have any degree of popular support."

State Department Situation Paper
Washington, D.C.
April 11, 1963

"I have exhausted myself in counseling my government to adopt more democratic and tolerant methods. Finally I could not do otherwise but resign."

Tran Van Chuong
South Vietnamese Ambassador to the United States
Washington, D.C.
August 22, 1963

"It is our hope that the political and military leadership that has now formed a new government in Viet-Nam [following the assasination of Diem on November 1] will be able to rally the country, consolidate the effort, get on with the job, so that the country can be independent and free and secure."

Dean Rusk
Secretary of State
Washington, D.C.
November 8, 1963

"The Military Revolutionary Council, considering the Provisional Constitution No. 1 dated Nov. 1, 1963 and considering that the Military Revolutionary Council established on Nov. 1,

1963, has proved to be ineffective in the face of an emergency in and out of the country;

"Decides after a vote:

"1. To terminate the mission of the executive committee of the Military Revolutionary Council set up on Nov. 1, 1963.

"2. To nominate Maj. Gen. Nguyen Khanh as chairman of the Military Revolutionary Council.

"3. That this decision be effective starting Jan. 30, 1964."

From text of declaration of military coup ousting
    Major General Duong Van Minh
Signed by General Khanh and forty-eight other army
    officers
Saigon, South Vietnam
January 30, 1964

"Khanh has the full . . . support of President Johnson and our whole government, and I want to let his people know this."

Robert S. McNamara
Secretary of Defense
South Vietnam
March 13, 1964

"General Khanh is on the right track . . ."

Dean Rusk
Secretary of State
Washington, D.C.
April 21, 1964

"As we have repeatedly made clear, a duly con-
stituted government exercising full power on the
basis of national unity and without improper in-
terference from any group, is the essential condi-
tion for the successful prosecution of the effort to
defeat the Vietcong and is the basis of United
States support for that effort."

State Department statement on military ouster of
  civilian Vietnamese government by South
  Vietnamese military
Washington, D.C.
December 22, 1964

"The Armed Forces Council, meeting in Saigon
on Jan. 23, 24, 26, and 27 resolved to rise up
boldly and accept its responsibility before history."

Declaration by Vietnamese Armed Forces Council
  that it was taking over the government
Saigon, South Vietnam
January 27, 1965

"We welcome the end of this interim period and look forward to close cooperation with this government."

Spokesman for United States Embassy in Vietnam greeting the ninth South Vietnamese Cabinet in sixteen months
Saigon, South Vietnam
February 17, 1965

"This is not a coup d'etat but it is a military operation.

"All units of the Army, Navy, and Air Force and Marines are contributing.

"We want to get rid of Khanh and restore order. We will see later if any of the present government will stay."

Colonel Pham Ngoc Thao
Leader of military group overthrowing General Khanh
Saigon, South Vietnam
February 19, 1965

142

"I think this [the overthrow of General Khanh] is unusual."

Lieutenant General Tran Thien Khiem
South Vietnamese Ambassador to the United States
Washington, D.C.
February 19, 1965

"We have capitulated."

Brigadier General Lam Van Phat
One of the leaders of the Pham Ngoc Thao coup that
    briefly ousted General Khanh
Saigon, South Vietnam
February 20, 1965

"This [the dismissal by the Armed Forces Council of General Khanh as commander in chief following his reinstatement after the Pham Ngoc Thao coup] is a good thing for my country. With Khanh we did not have stability, and without him we will have the stability we need."

Lieutenant General Tran Thien Khiem
South Vietnamese Ambassador to the United States
Washington, D.C.
February 21, 1965

"When we have the people's opinions on the constitution, we will prepare for real democratic elections in 1967. With these elections we will have legislative services according to the people's will, and a return elected by the people."

Nguyen Cao Ky
Premier of South Vietnam
Saigon, South Vietnam
January 15, 1966

"We will have an election as soon as possible."

Nguyen Cao Ky
Premier of South Vietnam
Saigon, South Vietnam
March 25, 1966

"[I have doubts about our ability] to go into a small, alien, undeveloped Asian nation and create stability where there is chaos, the will to fight where there is defeatism, democracy where there is no tradition of it and honest government where corruption is almost a way of life."

J. William Fulbright
Chairman of the Senate Foreign Relations Committee
Washington, D.C.
May 5, 1966

144

"The Saigon junta has ruled out 'neutralists,' has ruled out 'Communists,' has ruled out others of whom the generals disapproved, and now they will not even let those who are left participate freely and openly.

"Candidates have been barred because their view were 'unacceptable' though they were loyal citzens. The Saigon junta is making the elections a fraud and a farce."

Robert F. Kennedy
Senator from New York
Washington, D.C.
August 11, 1967

"If the National Assembly does not fulfill its duties [to purge three of its 'subversive members'], then the people and the army will assume the task to behead these Communists."

Nguyen Van Thieu
President of South Vietnam
Saigon, South Vietnam
November 11, 1969

"President Thieu and I repeatedly stated our willingness to accept the free decision of the South Vietnamese people. But we will not agree to the arrogant demand that the elected leaders of the government of Vietnam be overthrown before real negotiations begin."

Richard M. Nixon
President of the United States
San Clemente, California
April 20, 1970

12

Ho Chi Minh

"Ho Chi Minh is a Communist agent trained in Moscow . . . He is not representative of the nationalist aspirations of Viet Nam."

Philip C. Jessup
United States Ambassador-at-Large
Jakarta, Indonesia
February 2, 1950

"Ho Chi Minh is not followed by only Communists. He has succeeded in welding behind him a great lot of people, most of them nationalists. The Vietminh soldiers fought with a great faith, the faith of those who fight for the freedom and the sovereignty of their country."

General Christian de Castries
Commander of French Forces at Dienbienphu
Paris, France
September 16, 1954

"Ho Chi Minh is the symbol of nationalism in both parts of Divided Vietnam."

M. J. Desai
Indian Chairman of International Control Commission
   for Vietnam
New Delhi, India
December 30, 1954

"I have never talked or corresponded with a person knowledgeable in Indochinese affairs who did not agree that had elections been held as of the time of the fighting, possibly 80 percent of the population would have voted for the Communist Ho Chi Minh as their leader rather than Chief of State Bao Dai."

Dwight D. Eisenhower
Former President of the United States
Mandate for Change (1963)

"It is not McNamara's war; it is not the United States' war. It is Ho Chi Minh's war. Maybe it is Mao Tse-tung's war."

Dean Rusk
Secretary of State
Washington, D.C.
January 28, 1966

13

"America's Finest Hour"

"We know now that the Indo-China war is not merely a colonial problem but a fierce strategic struggle against despotism."

Dwight D. Eisenhower
General, United States Army
Coblenz, Germany
April 29, 1952

"The militant march of Communism has been halted."

Richard M. Nixon
Vice-President of the United States
Saigon, South Vietnam
July 6, 1956

"It was almost impossible to make the average Vietnamese peasant realize that the French, under whose rule his people had lived for some eighty years, were really fighting in the cause of freedom, while the Vietminh, people of their own ethnic origins, were fighting on the side of slavery."

Dwight D. Eisenhower
Former President of the United States
Mandate for Change (1963)

"Communist guerrilla warfare is waged without any declaration of war. In the case of Vietnam, it is waged from external sanctuaries which claim immunity to attack because the state which harbors them has not formally declared war."

Thomas J. Dodd
Senator from Connecticut
Washington, D.C.
February 23, 1965

"Only the Vietcong has committed atrocities in Vietnam."

Hubert H. Humphrey
Vice-President of the United States
Pittsburgh, Pennsylvania
May 13, 1965

"There are moments in human history when evil men and evil ways can be met only with force, and if good men give way, there is only the triumph of wickedness."

Richard Cardinal Cushing
Archbishop of Boston
Boston, Massachusetts
July 17, 1966

"Even though they [United States soldiers in Vietnam] bear arms and cause death and risk death, they are there as peacemakers."

Francis Cardinal Spellman
Archbishop of New York
New York City
August 21, 1966

"This war in Vietnam is, I believe, a war for civilization—certainly it is not a war of our seeking. It is a war thrust on us and we cannot yield to tyranny."

Francis Cardinal Spellman
Archbishop of New York
Saigon, South Vietnam
December 25, 1966

"American troops are the defense, protection and salvation not only of our country, but, I believe, of civilization itself."

Francis Cardinal Spellman
Archbishop of -New York
Danang, South Vietnam
December 26, 1966

"The American attitude toward the war is wholesome."

General William C. Westmoreland
Commander, United States Forces in South Vietnam
Honolulu, Hawaii
April 30, 1967

"We have actually written a new chapter in warfare."

General William C. Westmoreland
Army Chief of Staff
New Orleans, Louisiana
September 10, 1968

"I think that history will record that this may have been one of America's finest hours."

Richard M. Nixon
President of the United States
Saigon, South Vietnam
July 30, 1969

"A lot of guys feel that they [South Vietnamese civilians] aren't human beings. We just treated them like animals."

Michael Terry
Former private in the United States Army (Americal Division)
Quoted in the *London Times*
November 20, 1969

"There was about forty or forty-five people that we gathered in the center of the village . . . men, women, children . . . babies. And we all huddled them up . . . Lieutenant Calley . . . started shooting them. And he told me to start shooting. So I started shooting, I poured about four clips into the group . . . I fired them on automatic . . . you just spray the area . . . so you can't know how many you killed . . . I might have killed ten or fifteen of them . . . so we started to gather them up, more people, and we had seven or eight people . . . we put them in the hootch, and we dropped a hand grenade in there with them . . . they had about seventy or seventy-five people all gathered up. So we threw ours in with them and Lieutenant Calley . . . started pushing them off and shooting . . . off into the ravine. It was a ditch. And so we just pushed them off, and just started using automatics on them . . . men, women, children . . . and babies . . . after I done it, I felt good, but later on that day it was gettin' to me . . . It just seemed like it was the natural thing to do at the time . . ."

Paul Meadlo
Former private in United States Army (Americal Division)
Interview on CBS-TV
November 24, 1969

"We should be proud of our country because the Americal Division rules of engagement are based on Judeo-Christian traditions and are moral, unlike those of the enemy."

Lieutenant Colonel James E. Shaw
Chief Chaplain, Americal Division
Chulai, South Vietnam
November 29, 1969

"The only good Dink is a dead Dink."

James Farmer
Specialist 4 in United States Army (Americal
    Division)
Quoted in *New York Times*
Chulai, South Vietnam
November 29, 1969

"Vietnam has been good for the Marines, and the
Marines have been good for Vietnam."

Herman Nickerson, Jr.
Lieutenant General, U.S. Marine Corps
Danang, South Vietnam
March 9, 1970

"Our inquiry [into the Songmy incident] clearly
established that a tragedy of major proportions
occurred there on that day."

Lieutenant General William R. Peers
Head of Army panel investigating the Songmy
    incident
Washington, D.C.
March 17, 1970

"When men write the history of this nation, they will record that no people in the annals of time made greater sacrifices in a more selfless cause than the American people sacrificed for the right of eighteen million people in a faraway land to avoid the imposition of Communist rule against their will."

Richard M. Nixon
President of the United States
San Clemente, California
April 20, 1970

"I ask for your support for our brave men fighting tonight halfway around the world, not for territory, not for glory, but that their younger brothers and their sons and your sons can have a chance to grow up in a world of peace and freedom, and justice."

Richard M. Nixon
President of the United States
Washington, D.C.
April 30, 1970

"We expect the Soviets to protest this [attacks on enemy sanctuaries in Cambodia], just as we protested the Soviet invasion of Czechoslovakia."

Richard M. Nixon
President of the United States
As quoted by Senator Albert Gore
New York Times
May 6, 1970

"Before the Americans came to our rescue, we lived in quiet and peace. But now that you are here, all our people know is terror and bloodshed."

Unnamed Cambodian army captain
Chup, Cambodia
May 6, 1970

14

Plans to End the War

Negotiations

"France must seek a settlement based on negotiations."

Robert Schuman
Former French Foreign Minister
Paris, France
June 25, 1953

"It is impossible to lay down arms until victory is completely won."

Richard M. Nixon
Vice-President of the United States
Hanoi, Vietnam
November 4, 1953

"We cannot continue without hope and without aim to allow our youth to die."

> Pierre Mendès-France
> Paris, France
> February 12, 1954

"The United States will seek an honorable and peaceful settlement in Indo-China at the Geneva Conference but will oppose outright surrender to the Communists."

> Richard M. Nixon
> Vice-President of the United States
> Cincinnati, Ohio
> April 20, 1954

"The United States cannot afford any more compromises with the Communists, whether called neutralization or something else."

> Richard M. Nixon
> Former Vice-President of the United States
> Phu My, South Vietnam
> April 2, 1964

"History shows that the appeasers, the compromisers who refuse to stand up against aggression, have to take a stand sooner or later—and always at a less favorable time and place."

Richard M. Nixon
Former Vice-President of the United States
Reader's Digest
August, 1964

"However such proposals for negotiation under pressure may be explained or camouflaged by intricate rationales; it is simply a proposal to run up the white flag before the world and start running from Communism."

Everett M. Dirksen
Senate Minority Leader
Washington, D.C.
February 18, 1965

"There is, in my mind, little doubt that the conflict in Vietnam will end in the not-too-distant future in some form of compromised settlement that cannot help but lead to an eventual Communist take-over."

Melvin R. Laird
Representative from Wisconsin
Washington, D.C.
March 1, 1965

"We don't live in the clouds. That is why we have pleaded for years for a political solution. If we had that solution a few years ago, we would have had a perfectly neutralized South Vietnam and South Laos . . . [Events] served to demonstrate to the United States that I was right when I said in 1962 that unless you neutralize South Vietnam now it will be too late.

"Now we are in 1965 and it is too late.

"Even in the case of an American departure from South Vietnam, we shall never turn toward the Americans."

Prince Norodom Sihanouk
Chief of State of Cambodia
Pnompenh, Cambodia
March 6, 1965

"I am ready to go anywhere at any time and meet with anyone whenever there is promise of progress toward an honorable peace."

Lyndon B. Johnson
President of the United States
Washington, D.C.
March 25, 1965

"A conference not preceded by a verifiable Communist decision to cease attacking and subverting South Vietnam would be nothing more than a capitulation."

Henry Cabot Lodge
Former United States Ambassador to South Vietnam
Waltham, Massachusetts
March 31, 1965

"[The administration is] needlessly sacrificing American lives, if its only objective [is] to achieve a negotiated settlement establishing a coalition government with Communist representation."

Melvin R. Laird
Representative from Wisconsin
Washington, D.C.
June 14, 1965

"How much negotiations are you going to get unless they are beaten?"

Everett M. Dirksen
Senate Minority Leader
Washington, D.C.
January 7, 1966

"When you buy peace at any price it is always on the installment plan for another war."

Richard M. Nixon
Former Vice-President of the United States
New York City
January 29, 1966

"[There is] no reasonable possibility of a negotiated settlement . . . further discussion of a negotiated settlement delays the end of the war by simply encouraging the enemy that we are begging for peace."

Richard M. Nixon
Former Vice-President of the United States
Saigon, South Vietnam
August 7, 1966

"Allowing the Communists to help govern Vietnam cannot be squared with the President's stated policy of no reward for aggression."

Richard M. Nixon
Former Vice-President of the United States
New York City
November 3, 1966

"I know of no successful military effort that ever keyed its own intensity simply to match that of the aggressor—thus deliberately surrendering to the aggressor the initiative for major offensives."

Richard M. Nixon
Former Vice-President of the United States
New York City
November 3, 1966

"I do not want to get into a debate on a foreign policy meeting in Manila with a chronic complainer like Mr. Nixon . . . He never did really recognize and realize what was going on when he had an official position in the government."

Lyndon B. Johnson
President of the United States
Washington, D.C.
November 4, 1966

"Less than victory is inconceivable."

Francis Cardinal Spellman
Archbishop of New York
Saigon, South Vietnam
December 24, 1966

"The North Vietnamese and the Vietcong are not going to change their attitude by virtue of the U.S. protesting for peace . . . the only effective way . . . is to prosecute the war more effectively."

Richard M. Nixon
Former Vice-President of the United States
Green Bay, Wisconsin
February 5, 1968

"The administration may have overspoken when it said it would go any place, any time to start peace talks with North Vietnam . . . What everybody understood the President to mean was that the United States would go to a place that would be conducive to an honorable discussion, a reasonable peace."

Hubert H. Humphrey
Vice-President of the United States
Washington, D.C.
April 29, 1968

"We have to stop it with victory, or it will start all over again in a few years."

Richard M. Nixon
Former Vice-President of the United States
Good Housekeeping
July 1968

"We must unceasingly make clear to Hanoi that we do not seek nor will we accept a camouflaged surrender which would inevitably result in the United States writing off Southeast Asia."

Dwight D. Eisenhower
Former President of the United States
Miami Beach, Florida
July 30, 1968

"[The United States] swapped some of the greatest military concessions in the history of warfare for an enemy agreement on the shape of the bargaining table."

Spiro T. Agnew
Vice-President of the United States
Des Moines, Iowa
November 13, 1969

"We may still have time to negotiate a political settlement if we can bring ourselves to give up the untenable dream of an anti-Communist government in Saigon."

J. Williams Fulbright
Chairman of the Senate Foreign Relations Committee
Washington, D.C.
April 2, 1970

"If devotion to Thieu and Ky is the obstacle to a compromise political settlement, the asset we have is our remaining force of over 400,000 men in Vietnam—and our freedom to take them out. The Communists want them out, and it is supremely in our interests to get them out. That would seem a promising basis for doing business."

J. William Fulbright
Chairman of the Senate Foreign Relations Committee
Washington, D.C.
April 2, 1970

"I must report with regret that no progress has taken place on the negotiating front. The enemy still demands that we unilaterally and unconditionally withdraw all American forces, that in the process we overthrow the elected government of South Vietnam, and that the United States accept a political settlement that would have the practical consequence of the forceful imposition of a Communist government upon the people of South Vietnam.

"That would mean humiliation and defeat for the United States. This we cannot and will not accept."

Richard M. Nixon
President of the United States
San Clemente, California
April 20, 1970

"We will be conciliatory at the conference table, but we will not be humiliated. We will not be defeated."

Richard M. Nixon
President of the United States
Washington, D.C.
April 30, 1970

Vietnamization

"The President said that the Indochinese were people of small stature . . . and were not warlike."

Minutes of Far East discussions held by Roosevelt and Stalin
February 8, 1945

"We are trying to develop the national Vietnam army in order that we may one day bring back to Europe the greater part of the French Expedition-ary Force."

René Mayer
Premier of France
Paris, France
March 20, 1953

"You know it is the policy of my government to help those who help themselves—and the Vietnamese government is doing just that."

General Mark W. Clark
Commander, United States Forces in the Far East
Hanoi, Vietnam
March 23, 1953

"They [French officials] say this does not mean abandonment or withdrawal in a defeatist mood. It means gradual transfer of the defense from French to native troops accompanied by an effort to solve the Indo-Chinese war . . . by ultimate local negotiation."

Harold Callender
New York Times
Paris, France
July 21, 1953

"The Vietnamese National Army will soon assume much greater responsibility in the Indo-China war."

General Nguyen Van Hinh
Chief of Staff of Vietnamese National Army
Saigon, Vietnam
February 16, 1954

"Effective and aggressive training of Indo-Chinese troops is essential if the war is to be brought to a successful conclusion. We are willing to assist in such training in any practical way . . . such training in itself would not involve us in any way."

Charles E. Wilson
Secretary of Defense
Washington, D.C.
March 23, 1954

"The United States, on its part, agreed to contribute most of the required military end items and to finance most of the monetary cost of the program particularly in relation to training, equiping and maintaining more local forces."

John Foster Dulles
Secretary of State
Washington, D.C.
April 6, 1954

"The Vietnamese lack the ability to conduct a war by themselves or govern themselves."

Richard M. Nixon
Vice-President of the United States
Washington D.C.
April 16, 1954

"Before the end of the year, progress and development of our National Army will hold many surprises for you . . . you will see on the field of battle numerous divisions entirely Vietnamese under a National command."

General Nguyen Van Hinh
Chief of Staff of the Vietnamese National Army
Saigon, Vietnam
June 2, 1954

"This American mission will soon take charge of instructing the Vietnam army . . . The aim will be . . . to build a completely autonomous Vietnam army."

General J. Lawton Collins
United States Special Ambassador
Saigon, South Vietnam
November 17, 1954

"With a little more training, the Vietnamese army will be the equal of any other army in its ability to combat the enemy and will be able to defend itself against the Vietminh if attacked."

Wilbur M. Bruckner
Secretary of the Army
Saigon, South Vietnam
December 17, 1955

"One has to be here personally to sense the growing national character, the resistance of the Vietnamese people to the subversive insurgency threat. My overall impression is of a great national movement, assisted to some extent, of course, by Americans, but essentially a movement by Vietnamese to defend Vietnam against a dangerous and cruel enemy."

General Maxwell D. Taylor
United States Army Chief of Staff Designate
Saigon, South Vietnam
September 13, 1962

"I am confident the Vietnamese are going to win their war."

Admiral Harry D. Felt
Commander, United States Forces in the Pacific
Saigon, South Vietnam
January 11, 1963

"This intensification inevitably has carried us to the start of the road which leads to the point at which the conflict could become of greater concern and greater responsibility to the United States than it is to the government and people of South Vietnam.

"In present circumstances, pursuit of that course could involve an expenditure of American lives and resources on a scale which would bear little relationship to the interest of the United States or, indeed, to the interests of the people of Vietnam.

"If we are to avoid that course it must be clear to ourselves as well as to the Vietnamese where the primary responsibility lies in this situation. It must rest with the Vietnamese government and people. What further effort may be needed for the survival of the republic in present circumstances must come from that source.

"If it is not forthcoming, the United States can reduce its commitment or abandon it entirely, but there is no interest of the United States in Vietnam which would justify, in present circumstances, the conversion of the war in that country into an American war to be fought primarily with American lives."

Senate study, requested by President Kennedy
(Headed by Senator Mansfield)
Washington, D.C.
February 24, 1963

"We are prepared to continue to assist them, but I don't think that the war can be won unless the people support the effort, and in my opinion, in the last two months, the government has gotten out of touch with the people.

"In the final analysis, it's their war. They're the ones who have to win it or lose it. We can help them, give them equipment, we can send our men out there as advisors, but they have to win it, the people of Vietnam, against the Communists."

John F. Kennedy
President of the United States
Hyannis Port, Massachusetts
September 2, 1963

"We have completed the job of training South Vietnam's armed forces."

General Charles J. Timmes
Commander of United States Military Assistance
  Advisory Group in South Vietnam
Tokyo, Japan
October 31, 1963

"Of course it is not a question of a clear-cut victory over the Vietcong, but of getting the situation enough under control so the Vietnamese can carry on and take care of things alone."

General Paul D. Harkins
Commander of United States Military Assistance
    Command
Saigon, South Vietnam
November 13, 1963

"As the forces of your government become increasingly capable of dealing with this aggression, American military personnel in South Vietnam can be progressively withdrawn."

Lyndon B. Johnson
President of the United States
Letter to South Vietnamese Chief of State Duoung
    Van Minh
January 1, 1964

178

"Our first two years have been most eventful, and we have made significant progress in our program to advise and assist the Republic of Vietnam armed forces in their struggle against the Communist Vietcong."

General Paul D. Harkins
United States Army
Saigon, South Vietnam
February 8, 1964

"The contest in which South Vietnam is now engaged is first and foremost a contest to be won by the government and the people of that country for themselves. But those engaged in external direction and supply would do well to be reminded that this type of aggression is a deeply dangerous game."

Lyndon B. Johnson
President of the United States
Los Angeles, California
February 21, 1964

"In early October of last year I stated that I believed we should bring back U.S. personnel as they completed their training missions. I anticipated that the majority of the training missions could be completed by the end of 1965. I continue to believe that we should not leave an American in South Vietnam longer than necessary to train a Vietnamese counterpart to carry on that action."

Robert S. McNamara
Secretary of Defense
Washington D.C.
April 24, 1964

"Some others are eager to enlarge the conflict. They call upon us to supply American boys to do the job that Asian boys should do."

Lyndon B. Johnson
President of the United States
New York City
August 12, 1964

"We either have to get out or take some action to help the Vietnamese. They won't help themselves. We made a big mistake going in there, but I can't figure out any way to get out without scaring the rest of the world."

Richard B. Russell
Chairman of the Senate Armed Services Committee
Washington, D.C.
November 25, 1964

"The Vietnamese military forces continue to fight well. Our own military men consider most of them as tough and brave as any in the world."

William P. Bundy
Assistant Secretary of State for Far Eastern Affairs
Washington, D.C.
January 23, 1965

"He [Ambassador to South Vietnam, Maxwell D. Taylor] still contends that this is Vietnam's war, and he is probably technically correct."

George D. Aiken
Senator from Vermont
Washington, D.C.
June 11, 1965

"We are not there to substitute our efforts for
theirs. We are there to supplement their own
brave and gallant and continuing effort of defending themselves."

Lyndon B. Johnson
President of the United States
Washington, D.C.
August 12, 1965

"Asian problems should be solved by Asians."

Narciso Ramos
Foreign Minister of the Philippines

Adam Malik
Foreign Minister of Indonesia

Jakarta, Indonesia
August 23, 1966

"It is conceivable that within two years or less the
enemy will be so weakened that the Vietnamese
will be able to cope with a greater share of the war
burden. We will be able to phase down the level

of our military effort, withdraw some of our troops, with the understanding that the Vietnamese will be prepared to take over those functions that are being now performed by our troops."

General William C. Westmoreland
Commander, United States Forces in South Vietnam
Washington, D.C.
November 19, 1967

"The Vietcong are clearly getting protection from the population, and the so-called pacification program must be largely a sham."

Eugene J. McCarthy
Senator from Minnesota
Washington, D.C.
February 3, 1968

"The policy decision has been made to turn over gradually the major effort to the South Vietnamese."

Clark M. Clifford
Secretary of Defense
Washington, D.C.
April 11, 1968

"Pacification is entirely a government of South Vietnam operated program. We are only here in an advisory role."

Robert W. Komer
Civilian Administrator of American Pacification
  Program
Saigon, South Vietnam
July 6, 1968

"We would be badly mistaken if we think we can depend too much upon this South Vietnamese army winning this war or being able to hold the line.

"I don't believe they will be able to do it and I believe Hanoi knows this better than we do.

"We'll have to stay there for ten years at best."

John C. Stennis
Chairman of the Senate Armed Services Committee
Washington, D.C.
March 9, 1969

"The replacement of troops is not a one-year problem; it is a problem that will take years and years."

Nguyen Van Thieu
President of South Vietnam
Vungtau, South Vietnam
September 27, 1969

"President Nixon has a program to end the war in Vietnam. That program is Vietnamization."

Melvin R. Laird
Secretary of Defense
Washington, D.C.
October 29, 1969

"At the end of 1970 we will replace all American combat troops."

Nguyen Cao Ky
Vice-President of South Vietnam
Dalat, South Vietnam
November 5, 1969

"Vietnamization, of course, refers only to the assumption by the Vietnamese of that portion of the war effort carried on previously by the United States. It does not refer to the total war effort in which the South Vietnamese themselves have carried such a large and heavy burden for so many years."

Richard Capen
Defense Department spokesman
Washington, D.C.
November 19, 1969

"Our goal of course is to end the war in Vietnam, preferably by negotiation as quickly as possible—if not by negotiation, through Vietnamization in which the South Vietnamese will assume the primary responsibility for their own defense. We are moving on schedule on Vietnamization."

Richard M. Nixon
President of the United States
Washington, D.C.
January 30, 1970

"The assumptions regarding the present situation in Vietnam and the expected future course of developments in that country, on which U.S. policy is apparently based, seem to rest on far more ambiguous, confusing and contradictory evidence than pronouncements from Washington and Saigon indicate. The success of present American policy appears to depend on three factors: 1) The progressive Vietnamization of the military effort. 2) The stability and cohesiveness of the Thieu government. 3) The expectation that the enemy can and will do nothing to inhibit Vietnamization or disrupt the Thieu government's stability.

"There is, of course, an intimate relationship among these three factors. Indeed, it may be said that all must succeed—or, perhaps more accurately, that none may fail—if present U.S. objectives in Vietnam are to be realized . . .

"We believe that the evidence presented in this report leads to the inference that the prospects for a successful outcome of any one of the aforementioned three factors, much less all three, must be regarded as, at best, uncertain. Dilemmas thus seem to lie ahead in Vietnam, as they have

throughout our involvement in this war that appears to be not only far from won but far from
over."

   Conclusion of staff study by Senate Foreign Relations
      Committee
   Washington D.C.
   February 1, 1970

"Vietnamization is a semantic hoax—what it denotes is simply an extension of the Johnson foreign policy. It will not get us out of Vietnam; rather, it will perpetuate our involvement."

Harold E. Hughes
Senator from Iowa
Washington, D.C.
February 3, 1970

"Vietnamization has been a great public relations success, but it is not a true policy of disengagement.

"We have not Vietnamized the war, we have cosmetized it."

Charles E. Goodell
Senator from New York
Washington, D.C.
February 3, 1970

"Having failed to beat the Communists with a well-led, well-trained and superbly equipped American army of half a million men, we can hardly expect the ARVN on its own to do the job."

J. William Fulbright
Chairman of the Senate Foreign Relations Committee
Washington, D.C.
April 2, 1970

"[Vietnamization] is not working, and it is not likely to. The North Vietnamese have repeatedly asserted—and abundantly proven—that they are prepared to contest the swamp with us for as long as we choose to remain in it."

J. William Fulbright
Chairman of the Senate Foreign Relations Committee
Washington, D.C.
April 2, 1970

"Tonight I am pleased to report that progress in training and equipping South Vietnamese forces has substantially exceeded our original expectations last June."

Richard M. Nixon
President of the United States
San Clemente, California
April 20, 1970

"The decision I have announced tonight to withdraw 150,000 more men over the next year is based entirely on the progress of our Vietnamization."

Richard M. Nixon
President of the United States
San Clemente, California
April 20, 1970

". . . We should train and strengthen the Cambodian army."

Nguyen Van Thieu
President of South Vietnam
Saigon, South Vietnam
April 29, 1970

Withdrawal

"Both the Vietcong and the Americans have become too deeply engaged in South Vietnam to withdraw easily now.

"The Americans can keep things going as they are now in Vietnam for many years. But in the end America will get tired of the endless war and withdraw, leaving the field open for the Vietcong."

Prince Norodom Sihanouk
Chief of State of Cambodia
Kep, Cambodia
May 30, 1963

"Withdrawal of United States troops would be a great mistake."

John F. Kennedy
President of the United States
Hyannis Port, Massachusetts
September 2, 1963

"Secretary McNamara and General Taylor reported their judgment that the major part of the United States military task can be completed by 1965 although there may be a continuing requirement for a limited number of United States training personnel.

"They reported that by the end of this year the United States program for training Vietnamese should have progressed to the point where 1,000 United States military personnel assigned to South Vietnam can be withdrawn."

White House statement
Washington, D.C.
October 2, 1963

"If additional men are needed we'll send them. If others have completed their mission we'll withdraw them."

Lyndon B. Johnson
President of the United States
Washington, D.C.
March 7, 1964

"We will not withdraw, either openly or under the cloak of a meaningless agreement."

Lyndon B. Johnson
President of the United States
Baltimore, Maryland
April 17, 1965

"I am opposed to an unconditional withdrawal from Vietnam."

J. William Fulbright
Chairman of the Senate Foreign Relations Committee
Washington, D.C.
June 15, 1965

"If the United States cuts and runs in Vietnam we will have a temporary peace and then a certain world war."

Richard M. Nixon
Former Vice-President of the United States
Durham, N.C.
April 30, 1966

"Withdrawal or defeat in Vietnam would mean the beginning of the end for freedom in Asia."

Richard M. Nixon
Former Vice-President of the United States
Jackson, Mississippi
May 6, 1966

"The United States could well declare unilaterally that this stage of the Vietnam war is over, that we have 'won' in the sense that our armed forces are in control of most of the field and no potential enemy is in a position to establish its authority over South Vietnam."

George D. Aiken
Senator from Vermont
Speech in Senate
October 19, 1966

"Mutual withdrawal of North Vietnamese and United States troops simply turns back the clock two years and says 'Let the South Vietnamese fight it out with the Vietcong.'

"The South Vietnamese army could not prevail for any length of time over the Communist guerrillas without American advisors, air support and logistical backing. Communist victory would most certainly be the result if the North Vietnamese continued their own logistical support of the Communist guerrillas."

Richard M. Nixon
Former Vice-President of the United States
New York City
November 3, 1966

"The mutual withdrawal offer, which would ultimately allow the Vietcong to regain the upper hand, might be a temporarily successful propaganda bluff."

Richard M. Nixon
Former Vice-President of the United States
New York City
November 3, 1966

"If the United States withdrew from Vietnam, such an act may signal the beginning of an era of chaotic international relations for our nation.

"We would be truly rewarding aggression and terror.

"We would be proclaiming to the world that wars of national liberation can be successful and could not be stopped."

Daniel K. Inouye
Senator from Hawaii
Syracuse, N.Y.
December 7, 1966

"We are not ready to negotiate our defeat or a face-saving withdrawal."

General Earle G. Wheeler
Chairman, Joint Chiefs of Staff
Detroit, Michigan
December 18, 1967

"We are not going to be so soft-headed and pudding-headed as to say that we will stop our half of the war and hope and pray that they will stop theirs."

Lyndon B. Johnson
President of the United States
Washington, D.C.
December 19, 1967

"I believe that when the American people think this thing through, their final decision will be that these men must not have died in vain and that we must continue the fight.

"To pull out now under whatever guise would mean the end ultimately of all the free and independent countries of that area. You pull out our armed forces from South Vietnam and it will only be a question of time before every country up to the border of India falls under the Communist heel. That includes Laos and Cambodia—

right next door—as well as Thailand and Burma, and I'm not sure about India either, once they have got that far."

Dwight D. Eisenhower
Former President of the United States
Indio, California
December 22, 1967

"I don't see how pulling out without really meeting the problem of ending this thing is going to do other than cause us to fight the war again."

Spiro T. Agnew
Republican vice-presidential candidate
New York City
August 23, 1968

"Negotiations, or no negotiations, we could start to remove some American forces early in 1969."

Hubert H. Humphrey
Democratic presidential candidate
Philadelphia, Pennsylvania
September 9, 1968

"As far as the fighting forces are concerned, the requirements remain the same. There is no reduction, there will be no reduction until there is a change in the enemy's attitude.

"I don't want to pull the rug out from under our negotiators in Paris by indicating now that we are going to start cutting back our forces and leaving the enemy encouraged to believe that if they just wait, that they don't really have to negotiate now."

Richard M. Nixon
Republican presidential candidate
Denver, Colorado
September 25, 1968

"We would pull our troops back in a secondary position until we are absolutely certain that the local forces can take over the fighting."

Clark M. Clifford
Secretary of Defense
Washington, D.C.
September 29, 1968

"There is no prospect for a reduction of American forces in the foreseeable future."

Richard M. Nixon
President of the United States
Washington, D.C.
March 14, 1969

"We have no plans to reduce our troops until there is more progress."

Richard M. Nixon
President of the United States
Washington, D.C.
April 18, 1969

"I have decided to order the immediate redeployment from Vietnam of . . . 25,000 men."

Richard M. Nixon
President of the United States
Midway Island
June 8, 1969

"This must be just about the first time in the history of warfare that a nation has thought it could prevail by withdrawing combat troops and reducing its military presence."

Walter Lippmann
Newsweek Magazine
December 1, 1969

"The process of withdrawing American troops is going to continue; it's irreversible."

William P. Rogers
Secretary of State
Washington, D.C.
January 15, 1970

"We can now say with confidence that the South Vietnamese can develop the capability for their own defense, and we can say with confidence that all American combat forces can and will be withdrawn."

Richard M. Nixon
President of the United States
San Clemente, California
April 20, 1970

Military Solutions

"I think that 150,000 elite French troops should
have settled the issue in about four months."
>   General Douglas MacArthur
>   Commander, United States Forces in the Far East
>   Wake Island
>   October 15, 1950

"United States military officers do not seem fully
to understand the problems of guerrillas."
>   Unnamed member of staff of French General
>   Jean de Lattre de Tassigny
>   Washington, D.C.
>   September 15, 1951

"One of the most distressing statements I ever read is that of Governor Thomas Dewey of New York in his current book on Southeast Asia saying the Indo-China problem was purely military . . .

"If all popular forces were behind the ruling powers in Indo-China . . . the war should end in a matter of a few weeks."

William O. Douglas
Supreme Court Justice
Saigon, Vietnam
September 1, 1952

"I think that a military victory would be perhaps both possible and probable."

Charles E. Wilson
Secretary of Defense
Washington, D.C.
February 9, 1954

"Nobody could hope for a victory by arms. I think that the agreements concluded in Geneva were . . . the only logical end to the Indo-China war."

General Christian de Castries
Commander of French Forces at Dienbienphu
Paris, France
September 16, 1954

"Questions of defense, in a situation such as Vietnam, cannot be dealt with solely in military terms."

Dean Rusk
Secretary of State
Washington, D.C.
May 4, 1961

"We want the war to be won, the Communists to be contained, and our men to come home. We are not there to see a war lost."

John F. Kennedy
President of the United States
Washington, D.C.
September 12, 1963

"Why can't we make up our minds to win down there? We never hear the President say we will win, he only says we will contain them."

Barry Goldwater
Senator from Arizona
Stockton, California
March 18, 1964

"There can be no such thing as a purely 'military' solution to the war in South Viet-Nam."

Robert S. McNamara
Secretary of Defense
Washington, D.C.
March 26, 1964

"I agree with what I understand to be the administration's current attitude that the goal in Vietnam should be nothing less than victory. However, I am raising a question about whether the administration has a plan which is adequate to reach that goal."

Richard M. Nixon
Former Vice-President of the United States
Saigon, South Vietnam
April 3, 1964

"At this rough and dangerous stage there is no substitute for force and the will to use it, even though a total solution to the problem cannot be achieved solely by military means.

"I would not be surprised to see the Mekong Delta totally cleared of Communist guerrilla forces by the end of 1965."

Henry Cabot Lodge
United States Ambassador to South Vietnam
Life Magazine
April 17, 1964

"I'd drop a low-yield atomic bomb on the Chinese supply lines in North Vietnam."

Barry Goldwater
Senator from Arizona
Look Magazine
April 21, 1964

"We are not just down there as advisors, we are down there with our boys, and the boys are getting shot.

"Defoliation of the forests by low-yield atomic weapons could well be done."

Barry Goldwater
Senator from Arizona
Washington, D.C.
May 24, 1964

"As a President, I would say to my military people, 'How do we stop these supplies from coming down?' and we would do that."

Barry Goldwater
Senator from Arizona
San Diego, California
May 26, 1964

"All that is needed, in short, is the will to win—and the courage to use our power—now."

Richard M. Nixon
Former Vice-President of the United States
Reader's Digest
August 1964

"The choice here is either winning the war in South Vietnam or fighting a much bigger one in Southeast Asia. Now is the time to halt creeping Communist aggression."

Richard M. Nixon
Former Vice-President of the United States
Chicago, Illinois
October 7, 1964

"In the long run, there can be no military solution to the problems of Vietnam."

Lyndon B. Johnson
President of the United States
Washington, D.C.
May 4, 1965

"We know, as our adversaries should also know, that there is no purely military solution in sight for either side."

Lyndon B. Johnson
President of the United States
Washington, D.C.
May 13, 1965

"Let the military run the show."

Barry Goldwater
Former Senator from Arizona
Washington, D.C.
June 13, 1965

"It is clear to all reasonable Americans that a complete military victory in Vietnam, though theoretically attainable, can in fact be attained only at a cost far exceeding the requirements of our interest and our honor."

J. William Fulbright
Chairman of the Senate Foreign Relations Committee
Washington, D.C.
June 15, 1965

"Even though I am a military man, I don't think we can win the heart of the people just with a gun, but only by giving them a better way of life. That is obvious."

Nguyen Cao Ky
Premier of South Vietnam
Saigon, South Vietnam
August 31, 1965

"Sooner or later we, as free men, have to face the Chinese Communists. I think it is better to face them right now than in five or ten years."

Nguyen Cao Ky
Premier of South Vietnam
Washington, D.C.
July 25, 1966

"The Johnson administration said it was not seeking a military solution to the war, and it is now obviously seeking precisely that. It said it was there merely to help a legitimate government defend itself, and it has ended up by supporting a military clique that is not a government, not legitimate and is not really defending itself . . . It was not going beyond the seventeenth parallel in Vietnam, but it went beyond. It was merely going to respond to enemy attacks on its bases, but it went over to the offensive. It was not going to get involved in a major war on the Asian land mass, but it did.

"The President . . . said he would not negotiate, but then offered to do so . . . and even[in] this last adventure in Hanoi and Haiphong, we are told officially that these bombings are not an 'escalation' of the war."

James Reston
New York Times
Washington, D.C.
June 30, 1966

"President Eisenhower stuck to his basic position that if there was a solution in South Vietnam, it was political and not military insofar as the United States was concerned."

G.O.P. White Paper
Washington, D.C.
May 1, 1967

"Whatever happens in Vietnam, I can conceive of nothing except military victory."

Dwight D. Eisenhower
Former President of the United States
West Point, N.Y.
June 2, 1967

"We believe that . . . greater weight [should] be given to recommendations for military actions which our high-ranking military experts, with lifetimes of experience and expertise behind them, believe to be necessary to bring the war to a successful conclusion.

"Every military witness who testified emphasized that the air war has been waged under severe handicaps which were contrary to military principles.

"It is high time, we believe, to allow the military voice to be heard in connection with the tactical details of military operations."

Senate Preparedness Investigation Subcommittee
   report
Washington, D.C.
August 31, 1967

"The only way the United States could win a military victory over North Vietnam in the fore-seeable future is to commit genocide on that poor little country."

David M. Shoup
Former Commandant, U.S. Marine Corps
Washington, D.C.
December 18, 1967

"Short of destroying the entire country and its people, we cannot eliminate the enemy forces in Vietnam by military means; in fact, 'military victory' is no longer the U.S. objective. What should now also be recognized is that the opposing leadership cannot be coerced by the present or by any other available U.S. strategy into making the kinds of concessions currently demanded."

> Daniel Ellsberg
> Melvin Gurtov
> Oleg Hoeffding
> Arnold L. Horelick
> Konrad Kellen
> Paul F. Langer
> Staff Members of the Rand Corporation, all of whom have done research on Vietnam for the Federal Government
> Letter to the *New York Times* written as individuals and not in the capacity of Rand employees
> October 8, 1969

"Intensify the war. From a purely military point of view, this is what should be done. However, the intensification of the war at the present time is politically unsound. The war has been fought too long with political considerations overriding sound military judgment. Halting the bombing of North Vietnam was a great mistake, which gave a big advantage to the enemy.

"We may have to abandon the Vietnamization approach should the enemy fail to respond in due time to our efforts to end the war. In case we must later escalate the war, I believe that by resolute military action on our part, the enemy could be hurt to the point that he would move to fruitful peace talks.

"The sure way to maintain the peace is to be strong militarily and unafraid politically, and to let the enemy know that we will use that strength as necessary to maintain the security of the United States."

Mark W. Clark
Former United Nations Commander in Korea
Charleston, S.C.
February 20, 1970

"President Nixon has definitely made it his war. The risks are considerable. I hope and pray he can end the war this way [attacking enemy sanctuaries in Cambodia]."

Lee Metcalf
Senator from Montana
Washington, D.C.
April 30, 1970

"We know we can't win a ground war in Asia."

Spiro T. Agnew
Vice-President of the United States
Face the Nation (CBS-TV)
May 3, 1970

"The Exact Plan Must Be Kept Secret for Now'

"He [President Johnson] owes it to the people to come clean and tell them exactly what the plans are, the people should be told now, and not after the elections."

Richard M. Nixon
Former Vice-President of the United States
New York City
September 13, 1966

"My mission is to save the situation. The exact plan must be kept secret for now, you understand, but in principle it will bring peace with honor for everyone."

Nguyen Thanh Nam
"The Palm Tree Prophet"
(So named because of his twenty-year habit of sitting from dusk to dawn on top of a coconut palm praying to Buddha and Jesus)
Saigon, South Vietnam
December 10, 1966

"I pledge to you the new leadership will end the war and win the peace in the Pacific."

Richard M. Nixon
Former Vice-President of the United States
Nashua, N.H.
March 5, 1968

"If you know how to end the war and bring peace to the Pacific, Mr. Candidate, let the American people hear your formula now. Why wait until next year?"

Hubert H. Humphrey
Vice-President of the United States
Springfield, Illinois
March 8, 1968

"No one with this responsibility who is seeking office should give away any of his bargaining position in advance . . . Under no circumstances should a man say what he would do next January."

Richard M. Nixon
Former Vice-President of the United States
New York City
March 10, 1968

"Let's not destroy the chances for peace with a mouthful of words from some irresponsible candidate for President of the United States."

Richard M. Nixon
Former Vice-President of the United States
Evansville, Indiana
May 8, 1968

"I never meant to indicate there was a plan [to end the war]."

Spiro T. Agnew
Republican Vice-Presidential Candidate
Honolulu, Hawaii
September 21, 1968

15

The Silent Majority

"The government of Ngo Dinh Diem is popular
with a silent majority and is criticized only by a
noisy minority of the population."

Mme. Ngo Dinh Nhu
Sister-in-law of President Ngo Dinh Diem
Saigon, South Vietnam
August 7, 1963

"This is no time for consensus government. It's a
time for leadership. The average citizen doesn't
know what the stakes are in Vietnam."

Richard M. Nixon
Former Vice-President of the United States
Los Angeles, California
February 11, 1965

THE SILENT CENTER MUST SPEAK UP!

"The great majority of our people have been silent too long; their voices must now be heard."

Freedom House advertisement
New York Times
July 25, 1965

"We are naturally aware of various noisy demonstrations that have taken place and are scheduled to take place, but I would like to point out that these groups constitute an infinitesimal faction of the American people, the vast majority of whom have indicated their strong support of President Johnson's policy in Vietnam."

Robert J. McCloskey
State Department spokesman
Washington, D.C.
October 15, 1965

"There will be some nervous nellies and some who will become frustrated and bothered and break ranks under the strain."

Lyndon B. Johnson
President of the United States
Chicago, Illinois
May 17, 1966

"AN OBLIGATION TO SHOUT"

"The consensus, which is clear to all experienced observers, must not be obscured by the behavior of a small segment of our population. They have the right to be heard, but they impose on the rest of us the obligation to make unmistakably clear the nation's firm commitment."

Statement by Freedom House
Signed by Richard M. Nixon and 104 other national
   figures
November 28, 1965

"The Pentagon and State Department are running out of excuses, so now they are blaming the failure of their policy on those who warned all along that it wouldn't work."

George McGovern
Senator from South Dakota
Washington, D.C.
December 19, 1967

"North Vietnam cannot defeat or humiliate the United States. Only Americans can do that."

Richard M. Nixon
President of the United States
Washington, D.C.
November 3, 1969

"So tonight, to you, the great silent majority of my fellow Americans, I ask for your support."

Richard M. Nixon
President of the United States
November 3, 1969

"[Winston Churchill] didn't have to contend with a gaggle of commentators raising doubts about ... whether Britain had the stamina to see the war through."

Spiro T. Agnew
Vice-President of the United States
Des Moines, Iowa
November 13, 1969

"They've got an invisible program to end an undeclared war backed by a silent majority."

1970 Senators for Peace and New Priorities
Advertisement placed in the *New York Times*
February 27, 1970

"You know, you see these bums, you know, blowing up the campuses. Listen, the boys on the college campuses today are the luckiest people in the world—going to the greatest universities—and here they are burning up the books. I mean storming around about this issue, I mean you name it, get rid of the war, there'll be another one."

Richard M. Nixon
President of the United States
Addressing Pentagon employees
Washington, D.C.
May 1, 1970

16

Laos

"We cannot let Laos fall to the Communists even if we have to fight."

Dwight D. Eisenhower
President of the United States
Washington, D.C.
December 31, 1960

"Under what authority are United States Air Force and United States Navy planes, flown by American pilots, bombing the Plain of Jars which is hundreds of miles from the Ho Chi Minh Trail and has nothing to do with the war in Vietnam?"

Eugene J. McCarthy
Senator from Minnesota
Washington, D.C.
February 19, 1970

"I do not see how we are going to get out of that situation [in Vietnam] by getting involved in another war."

John Sherman Cooper
Senator from Kentucky
Washington, D.C.
February 25, 1970

"It would be a cruel disappointment of President Nixon's hopes if the success of Vietnamization in South Vietnam depends on escalation of the United States engagement in Laos.

"If that has become a new element of the conflict in Southeast Asia, then the American policy should be fully reappraised.

"For I believe that the American people—and the Congress—will not ultimately accept a withdrawal policy that entails merely a changing of uniforms and titles and a re-engagement in Laos."

Charles McC. Mathias, Jr.
Senator from Maryland
Washington, D.C.
February 25, 1970

Goldwater: "Does the Senator mean that the United States has troops in combat in Laos?"

Symington: "It depends on a definition."

Goldwater: "I mean Americans engaged in fighting on the ground."

Symington: "I am not in a position to answer any questions . . . in open session at this time . . . because the transcript has not been released as yet on any meaningful basis . . ."

Goldwater: "The reason I ask is that it has not been any secret that we have been flying fighter-support missions in support of the Laotian army up on the Plaine des Jarres. The Senator, I know, has known about that for a long time. If the information is classified, I will not press the point . . ."

Exchange in the Senate between Senator Stuart Symington and Senator Barry Goldwater
Washington, D.C.
February 25, 1970

"The President has made it very clear that should any decision be made, or a recommendation on his part be made as far as the use of American military ground combat forces in Laos, that he would come to the Congress of the United States for such approval."

Melvin R. Laird
Secretary of Defense
Washington, D.C.
February 26, 1970

"We have no present plans, if [Laos] is overrun, to use combat troops. I do not want to say that we would never think about it. But there are no present plans of that kind."

William P. Rogers
Secretary of State
Washington, D.C.
March 3, 1970

"We have continued to conduct air operations. Our first priority for such operations is to interdict the continued flow of troops and supplies across Laotian territory on the Ho Chi Minh Trail. As Commander in Chief of our armed forces, I consider it my responsibility to use our air power to interdict this flow of supplies and men into South Vietnam and thereby avoid a heavy toll of American and allied lives.

"In addition to air operations on the Ho Chi Minh Trail, we have continued to carry out reconnaissance flights in North Laos and fly combat-support missions for Laotian forces when requested to do so by the Royal Laotian Government.

"In every instance our combat air operations have been increased only as the number of North Vietnamese in Laos and the level of their aggression has increased."

Richard M. Nixon
President of the United States
Key Biscayne, Florida
March 6, 1970

"When requested by the Royal Laotian Government, we have continued to provide military assistance to regular and irregular Laotian forces in the form of equipment, training and logistics. The levels of our assistance have risen in response to the growth of North Vietnamese combat activities."

Richard M. Nixon
President of the United States
Key Biscayne, Florida
March 6, 1970

"Our goal in Laos has been and continues to be to reduce American involvement and not to increase it, to bring peace in accordance with the 1962 accords and not to prolong the war."

Richard M. Nixon
President of The United States
Key Biscayne, Florida
March 6, 1970

"There are no American ground combat troops in Laos.

"We have no plans for introducing ground combat forces into Laos.

"No American stationed in Laos had ever been killed in ground combat operations."

Richard M. Nixon
President of the United States
Key Biscayne, Florida
March 6, 1970

"Captain Bush was in his quarters, in the compound ten miles to the rear of the expected line of contact with the enemy [in Laos], when North Vietnamese commandos attacked the compound. Captain Bush took action immediately to attempt to protect other persons in the compound, exposing himself to enemy fire, and was killed.

"He was not engaged in combat operations . . . [he died as a result of] hostile action."

Gerald L. Warren
Deputy Presidential Press Secretary
Key Biscayne, Florida
March 8, 1970

"Effective immediately [the Department of Defense will] inform the American public about all American aircraft losses and military air personnel casualties once search and rescue missions are completed . . .

"This clearly shows the intent of the President to inform the American people of the scope of United States involvement in Laos and his intention to keep the American people fully informed."

Ronald L. Ziegler
Presidential Press Secretary
Washington, D.C.
March 9, 1970

"[President Nixon] is bending over backwards to avoid any credibility crisis in Laos."

Frank Shakespeare
Director, U.S. Information Agency
New York City
March 10, 1970

"The President does not have authority, nor has
Congress given him authority, to engage in combat operations in Laos, whether on the land, in
the air or from the sea."

J. William Fulbright
Chairman of the Senate Foreign Relations Committee
Washington, D.C.
March 11, 1970

"If a situation should arise that would require
consideration of combat forces in Laos, I told the
Senate of the United States that we would consult
with them to the fullest extent possible."

William P. Rogers
Secretary of State
Washington, D.C.
March 17, 1970

17

Cambodia

"A showdown between the extreme right wing and myself is most probable.

"A coup d'etat is possible, unless I step down before they depose me. Everything is possible. I may be beaten. I do not like civil war. I do not want to see bloodshed among my compatriots.

"[Many army officers] are nostalgic about American aid, which would enable them to lead an easy life.

"The Americans are inside the castle walls— that is, inside our homes . . . whether through the embassy, the C.I.A. or any such like organization, I do not know.

"[If the right wing takes over] at best Cambodia would be a second Thailand and at worst it would be a second Laos or South Vietnam.

"I do not want to see that happen."

Prince Norodom Sihanouk
Chief of State of Cambodia
Paris, France
March 12, 1970

"The first feelers for the extension of military aid have already been sent abroad by the new government in Cambodia. There is no blinking at the fact that it is to this nation that the Cambodian aid appeal is addressed."

Mike Mansfield
Senate Majority Leader
Washington, D.C.
March 31, 1970

"It seems to us that our best policy is to be as quiet as possible, to avoid any act which appears to violate the neutrality of Cambodia. That is why we have discouraged cross-border operations. That is why we have cautioned against skirmishes on the border.

"We have cautioned the South Vietnamese on that subject. We have made it clear we think it is inadvisable to have cross-border operations now."

William P. Rogers
Secretary of State
Transcript of report to Senate Foreign Relations
    Committee
April 2, 1970

"I am apprehensive of our ability to stay out of war in Laos and Cambodia as long as we remain at war in Vietnam . . . The Communists are not going to confine the fight to a battlefield of our choosing, and, as Secretary Rogers readily admitted, the initiative is theirs."

J. William Fulbright
Chairman of the Senate Foreign Relations Committee
Washington, D.C.
April 2, 1970

"No U.S. advisers have gone into Cambodia."
  United States military spokesman
  Quoted in the *New York Times*
  Pnompenh, Cambodia
  April 17, 1970

"We consider the massacre of innocent civilians
[in Cambodia] to be abhorrent and to be actions
that warrant condemnation."
  Ronald L. Ziegler
  Presidential Press Secretary
  Washington, D.C.
  April 17, 1970

"Maybe a few soldiers did kill some Vietcong
terrorists who infiltrated into Cambodia to stir up
trouble. Perhaps a few Cambodian soldiers killed.
In every army there are some black sheep."
  Kihm Tit
  Cambodian delegate to the United Nations
  New York City
  April 17, 1970

"At this point, I think the best we can hope for is the equivalent of the military situation that prevailed before the coup. Our chances of making much real capital out of the situation seem to be diminishing rapidly."

Unnamed American military official
Quoted in the *New York Times*
Saigon, South Vietnam
April 19, 1970

"Almost 40,000 Communist troops are now conducting overt aggression against Cambodia, the small neutralist country that the Communists have used for years as a base for attack on South Vietnam in violation of the Geneva Accords of 1954."

Richard M. Nixon
President of the United States
San Clemente, California
April 20, 1970

"But I again remind the leaders of North Vietnam that while we are taking these risks for peace [withdrawing 150,000 more troops in the next year], they will be taking grave risks should they attempt to use the occasion to jeopardize the security of our remaining forces in Vietnam by increased military action in Vietnam, in Cambodia or in Laos."

Richard M. Nixon
President of the United States
San Clemente, California
April 20, 1970

"We recognize that if we escalate and we get involved in Cambodia with our ground troops that our whole program is defeated."

William P. Rogers
Secretary of State
Testimony before House Appropriations Subcommittee
April 23, 1970

[The Vietnamese Communist offensive in Cambodia is] "a foreign invasion of a neutral country which cannot be considered in any way a pretense of a civil war."

Ronald L. Ziegler
Presidential Press Secretary
Washington, D.C.
April 24, 1970

Secretary Rogers: "The President has the problem: Do you continue fighting the war in a way that doesn't make sense, or do you change it?"

Senator Symington. "I thought we were going to stop the war, not change it."

Transcript of Proceedings
Senate Foreign Relations Committee
Washington, D.C.
April 27, 1970

"This [South Vietnamese attacks on enemy sanctuaries in Cambodia] could be a turning point in the war for us for the good. I do not believe in itself it is an escalation—not yet, not yet."

John C. Stennis
Senator from Mississippi
Washington, D.C.
April 29, 1970

"The Secretary [William P. Rogers] feels that he, in his appearance on Monday afternoon before the committee, answered questions honestly and in light of the circumstances at the time."

Robert J. McCloskey
State Department spokesman
Washington, D.C.
April 29, 1970

"To protect our men who are in Vietnam and to guarantee the continued success of our withdrawal and Vietnamization program I have concluded that the time has come for action . . . Tonight American and South Vietnamese units will attack the headquarters for the entire Communist military operation in South Vietnam . . . This is not an invasion of Cambodia . . . our purpose is not to occupy the areas . . . We take this action not for the purpose of expanding the war into Cambodia but for the purpose of ending the war in Vietnam, and winning the just peace we all desire."

Richard M. Nixon
President of the United States
Washington, D.C.
April 30, 1970

"A week ago I never thought I'd be in Cambodia. I suppose we're making history, but as far as I can see, Cambodia is no different from Vietnam."

Sergeant Carl Holzschub
Landing Zone X-Ray
Cambodia
May 1, 1970

"I can't believe it."

Prince Norodom Monissara
Secretary General of the Cambodian Foreign Ministry
Commenting on President Nixon's speech announcing
   attacks on enemy sanctuaries in Cambodia
May 1, 1970

Index

Agnew, Spiro T., 97, 116, 166, 198, 217, 220, 225
Aiken, George D., 180, 194
Ball, George W., 7
Beebe, George, 8
Bruckner, Wilbur M., 173
Bundy, William P., 33, 50, 118, 119, 180
Bunker, Ellsworth, 42, 85, 86, 127
Burdick, Usher L., 17
Callender, Harold, 170
Capen, Richard, 185
Chapman, Leonard F., Jr., 115
Chuong, Tran Van, 138
Clark, Mark W., 170, 216
Clifford, Clark M., 124, 182, 199
Collins, J. Lawton, 64, 134, 172
Cooper, John Sherman, 228
Cushing, Richard Cardinal, 151

de Castries, Christian, 71, 147, 204
Dejean, Maurice, 66
Desai, M. J., 147
de Tassigny, Jean de Lattre, 46, 63, 64
Dewey, Thomas E., 46
Dillon, C. Douglas, 54
Dirksen, Everett M., 160, 163
Dodd, Thomas J., 50, 150
Don, Tran Van, 76
Dong, Pham Van, 130, 131
Dong, Vuong Van, 137
Douglas, William O., 203
Dulles, John Foster, 17, 47, 48, 67, 69, 71, 72, 128, 171
Eisenhower, Dwight D., 13, 14, 15, 17, 29, 36, 48, 52, 68, 73, 148, 149, 150, 166, 198, 212, 227
Ellsberg, Daniel, 41, 215
Ely, Paul, 68
Erskine, Graves B., 13

Farmer, James, 155

Felt, Harry D., 74, 174

Fulbright, J. William, 41, 43, 44, 58, 104, 106, 143, 167, 189, 193, 209, 235, 238

Galbraith, John Kenneth, 51, 81

Gavin, James M., 108, 114

Goldwater, Barry, 27, 32, 79, 110, 205, 206, 207, 209, 229

Goodell, Charles E., 188

Goodwin, Richard N., 56

Gore, Albert, 106

Griffin, Robert Allen, 62

Gurtov, Melvin, 41, 215

Habib, Philip C., 122

Hanh, Nguyen Huu, 74

Harkins, Paul D., 76, 177, 178

Heath, Donald R., 65

Hinh, Nguyen Van, 170, 172

Ho Chi Minh, 63, 131

Hoeffding, Oleg, 41, 215

Holzschub, Carl, 244

Horlick, Arnold L., 41, 215

Hughes, Harold E., 188

Humphrey, Hubert H., 23, 42, 81, 150, 165, 198, 219

Inouye, Daniel K., 196

Javits, Jacob K., 25

Jenner, William E., 16

Jessup, Philip C., 3, 30, 146

Johnson, Lyndon B., ii, 4, 33, 36, 55, 77, 82, 83, 89, 90, 99, 102, 105, 111, 117, 118, 119, 120, 121, 125, 132, 162, 164, 177, 178, 179, 181, 192, 193, 197, 208, 223

Katzenbach, Nicholas deB., 106

Kellen, Konrad, 41, 215

Kennedy, John F., 3, 20, 70, 176, 191, 204

Kennedy, Robert F., 38, 75, 91, 115, 144

Khiem, Tran Thien, 142

Khrushchev, Nikita, 75

Knowland, William F., 14, 16, 18

Komer, Robert W., 87, 95, 183

Ky, Nguyen Cao, 39, 80, 82, 143, 184, 210

Laird, Melvin R., 10, 117, 161, 162, 184, 230

Lam, Hoang Xuam, 125

Langer, Paul F., 41, 215

Langer, William, 54

LeMay, Curtis, 111

Lippmann, Walter, 201

Lodge, Henry Cabot, 77, 162, 206

McCarthy, Eugene J., 12, 90, 182, 227

McCloskey, Robert J., 24, 25, 222, 243
McGovern, George, 224
McMahon, Richard A., 94
McNamara, Robert S., 21, 23, 27, 31, 32, 59, 76, 82, 85, 90, 100, 101, 107, 110, 113, 139, 179, 205
MacArthur, Douglas, 202
MacDonald, Malcolm, 68
Malik, Adam, 181
Mansfield, Mike, 237
Mathias, Charles McC., Jr., 228
Mayer, René, 169
Meadlo, Paul, 154
Mendés-France, Pierre, 133, 159
Metcalf, Lee, 217
Monissara, Prince Norodom, 244
Morse, Wayne, 30, 60, 100, 109
Moss, John E., 7
Muskie, Edmund S., 96
Nam, Nguyen Thanh, 218
Navarre, Henri-Eugene, 67, 72
Nhu, Mme. Ngo Dinh, 221
Nickerson, Herman, Jr., 155
Nixon, Richard M., 12, 16, 19, 28, 37, 39, 40, 43, 44, 45, 49, 50, 66, 70, 78, 80, 81, 83, 96, 123, 135, 145, 149, 152, 156, 157, 158, 159, 160, 163, 164, 165, 166, 168, 172, 185, 190, 193, 194, 195, 199, 200, 201, 205, 207, 208, 218, 219, 220, 221, 224, 226, 231, 232, 233, 240, 241, 243
O'Daniel, John W., 18, 72
Peers, William R., 155
Phat, Lam Van, 142
Pineau, Christian, 15
Radford, Arthur W., 64, 69
Ramos, Narciso, 181
Reischauer, Edwin O., 92
Reston, James, 5, 211
Robertson, Walter S., 73, 135
Robinson, Douglas, 125
Rogers, William P., 116, 201, 230, 235, 238, 241
Romney, George, 10
Rusk, Dean, ii, 31, 55, 56, 57, 58, 61, 79, 83, 98, 138, 140, 148, 204
Russell, Richard B., 107, 180
Safer, Morley, 9
Salan, Raoul, 65
Schlesinger, Arthur M., Jr., 37
Schuman, Robert, 158
SEATO Treaty, 53
Shakespeare, Frank, 234

248

Shank, Edwin G., Jr., 22
Sharp, U.S. Grant, 86
Shaw, James E., 154
Shoup, David M., 52, 61, 101, 115, 214
Sihanouk, Prince Norodom, 38, 59, 66, 75, 161, 191, 236
Sparkman, John A., 119
Spellman, Francis Cardinal, 151, 152, 165
Stennis, John C., 15, 183, 242
Sylvester, Arthur, 76
Symington, Stuart, 229
Taylor, Maxwell D., 21, 37, 108, 109, 173
Terry, Michael, 153
Thao, Pham Ngoc, 141
Thieu, Nguyen Van, 88, 126, 144, 184, 190

Thompson, Sir Robert, 95
Timmes, Charles J., 176
Tit, Kihm, 239
Treaster, Joseph B., 126
Truman, Harry S., 63
Wagner, Robert, 136
Waier, Alex, 112
Warren, Gerald L., 233
Westmoreland, William C., 29, 60, 84, 85, 87, 89, 92, 93, 110, 116, 121, 152, 181
Wheeler, Earle G., 95, 196
Whitten, Jamie L., 94
Williams, Samuel T., 19
Wilson, Charles E., 171, 203
Young, Stephen M., 11
Ziegler, Ronald L., 234, 239, 242

Born in New York, WILLIAM G. EFFROS now lives in Philadelphia, where he owns a management consulting firm called TH INC. Since graduating from Antioch College, Mr. Effros has been in the printing business, has devised a computer program for mating dogs, and continues to work as a free-lance writer. Mr. Effros is twenty eight years old and married.